WHO SHOULD RUN THE UNIVERSITIES?

First in the third series of Rational Debate Seminars
sponsored by the American Enterprise Institute
held at
The Madison Hotel
Washington, D.C.

WHO SHOULD RUN THE UNIVERSITIES

John A. Howard
H. Bruce Franklin

RATIONAL DEBATE SEMINARS

American Enterprise Institute
for Public Policy Research
Washington, D.C.

FOREWORD

One of the truly transcendent questions for this generation has become "Who Should Run the Universities?" The American Enterprise Institute has been pleased to provide two radically different answers to this question in its first Rational Debate of the current academic year, held in January at the Madison Hotel in Washington, D.C.

Dr. John Howard, president of Rockford College, presents what might be termed one of the orthodox solutions, while the self-professed Marxist revolutionary, H. Bruce Franklin, advocates an admittedly minority but provocative one.

As in its previous two Rational Debate seasons, the American Enterprise, Institute hopes in this way to make its contribution to the national dialogue on another important public policy issue of concern to all levels of our leadership.

April 15, 1969   William J. Baroody
          President
          American Enterprise Institute
           for Public Policy Research

PREFACE

As this debate was being presented on three successive Thursdays in January, 1969, militant students were pressing their demands for change on campuses at San Francisco State, the University of California at Berkeley, and Brandeis University. In the calm of a conference room at the Madison Hotel in the nation's capital, some of the pros and cons of these campus confrontations, student-faculty versus faculty-administration, were sorted out and examined. As in any human endeavor, the canvass of alternatives was not exhaustive, perhaps, but the participants were sincere in seeking solutions to one of the major conundrums of the 1960s: Who Should Run the Universities? Divided as the two principals in the Rational Debate were, disparit as the suggestions from the panel were in the discussion periods, there was an unmistakable sense of movement. American education is still—or once again, some say—on the march. For all the ruckus on campus, despite all the attention given to the daily din, there has been too little questioning of where American education is marching.

President Howard and Professor Franklin have very different destinations in mind, as they both made clear. This Rational Debate, the first of this third season under sponsorship of the American Enterprise Institute, should serve as an awakening. Do we see clearly the next fork in the road, and the very different worlds that await us, depending on which fork we choose?

Once again the American Enterprise Institute has provided us with basic material for sober evaluation of our prospects in one of the most fundamental fields, the education of future generations of American leaders, the probable inheritors of a world-trusteeship role unprecedented in the history of mankind.

April 14, 1969   G. Warren Nutter
Coordinator
Rational Debate Series

CONTENTS

FIRST LECTURE

JOHN A. HOWARD

A story is revived each Christmas season about a
mother who is attracted by a do-it-yourself toy
comprised of brightly-colored levers, gears, circuits,
connector arms, and other fascinating mechanical
paraphernalia. When the clerk comes up, the mother
says, regretfully, that she supposes the toy is too
complicated for her son, he could never put it together
properly. "But, Madam," replies the clerk, "that is
precisely why it is such a valuable educational toy. It
can't be made to work. And what will better prepare
a youngster to live in the real world?"

Anyone engaged in examining and evaluating the
American university today is tempted to conclude that
the university is very much like the toy. It is thought
to prepare the young person for life, but it is impossible
to put it together so that it will work.

The literature on the subject of the present debate
is already extensive, and has been multiplying swiftly
since the Berkeley incidents in the spring of 1964.
I do not propose to rehash what has already been well
phrased by many bright and lofty spokesmen. Serious

students of the question should certainly consider the statements in the fall, 1968, issue of the *Educational Record*, also a publication of the American Council on Education, *The Future Academic Community: Continuity and Change*, a new book by Jacques Barzun, *The American University*, and the January, 1969, issue of *Fortune* magazine. My endeavor will be to re-examine the purpose of the university, to challenge some of the basic assumptions on which the academic community now seems to operate, and to suggest the distribution of power and the qualifications of those chosen for power which will most likely deliver on the purposes identified.

Two preliminary clarifications are needed. For this paper, I shall use the term, "university" to mean those institutions which grant the baccalaureate degree. Further, the matter of "running" a university suggests a simplicity of operation that doesn't exist in a complex human institution. A university is not like a locomotive where the engineer actually makes the decisions and manipulates the equipment to run the train. Since the verb is central to the sense of our discussion, I shall define "run" in these remarks to mean, having and utilizing the power to make the most important decisions affecting the university.

In order to make sensible recommendations about who should run the university, we really have to identify what the university is to accomplish. Stanford's President Sterling was once asked in a public

meeting whether he thought Stanford would ever run
the United States government as Harvard was running
it in the Kennedy Administration. "That," he said,
"would depend entirely on the direction in which the
United States was running."

We have to know where the university is running
to before we can determine who should run it.

The dominant concept of the university mission is
rather simple. McGeorge Bundy in an article in *The
Atlantic Monthly* said, "Nothing in the corporate
claim of the institution can outweigh the preeminent
requirement that its teachers and scholars should be
free to do their own best work as they themselves
determine." A three-year study conducted by the
U.S. Office of Education surveyed 7,500 professors
and administrators at 68 nondenominational institutions as to what *are* the top ten goals of the university
and what they *should be*. The results reported last
April proclaimed the number one objective, ideally
and in actuality, to be "Protect the faculty's right to
academic freedom."

Among the other nine goals found on either list,
there is none relating to student conduct or student
attitudes except, of course, conduct and attitudes
pertaining to scholarship. In July of this year, *Time*
magazine quoted the distinguished educational theorist,
Dr. Lewis B. Mayhew, in his presidential address to
the American Association for Higher Education as
follows: "Colleges are not churches, clinics, or even

parents. Whether or not a student burns a draft card, participates in a civil rights march, engages in pre-marital or extra-marital sexual activity, becomes pregnant, attends church, sleeps all day or drinks all night, is not really the concern of an educational institution."

The present orthodoxy is that the university is to extend the limits of man's knowledge and sharpen the intellectual processes of the student and store the student's mind with knowledge. All this is sometimes more compactly phrased as the "pursuit of truth."

I would like to suggest that we are in error in thus restricting the mission of education, and it is the grave and far-reaching consequences of this error which have brought about confusion within the university, and confusion about the university, so great that intelligent men will gather for a discussion such as this.

Knowledge, of itself, has no value. It is only the use to which man puts his knowledge that gives it value. By treating the pursuit of knowledge as the noblest endeavor and a self-justifying endeavor and one which must never be confined, we have lost track of the meaning and the consequences of the educational process. It is a remarkable lack of perception which permits the academic freedom of the faculty to displace a concern for what happens to the student as the first order of business in the educational process.

Under present definitions and policies, the university may just as readily graduate an Adolph Hitler as an Albert Schweitzer, a bright charlatan as readily as a bright saint.

Most of the college student eruptions in the last four years have been directly related in one way or another to the professional neutrality of the university on all issues. Students are demanding that the university abandon its neutrality, take sides and take action concerning the great moral issues of our times. Students have demanded that the universities withdraw from the Institute for Defense Analysis and prohibit recruiters from the military services and recruiters from the manufacturers of napalm and refuse to do business with commercial enterprises which support South Africa.

Students have also played on the other side of the fence. As well as attacking the university for its refusal to make institutional value judgments, students have attacked it for its failure to live up to its enunciated valueless posture. If the university takes no position, then, they say, it should abandon value judgments about student conduct. Students have demanded that rules governing the use of alcohol, drugs, bedroom visitation, and other limits on student actions be rescinded.

The amazing thing is that some universities have ceded ground in both directions. Such administrative inconsistency added to the university's subordination of concern for the students to a concern for scholarly productivity has given rise to the third area of student militancy, the demand for student power in the making of university decisions.

In almost every society, save ours, those vested with authority have clearly seen that education does have consequences for the student, that the success of a society is wholly dependent upon an educational system which consciously, and as the highest priority, prepares the youth to live in that kind of society. A great society or a good society cannot be created by enlightened legislation and enormous amounts of money and tens of thousands of well-intentioned employees busily working in great society programs. A good society can only be created by good citizens. If the highest priority of our educational system is to have every faculty member do his own thing without limits and without regard to the views or the interests of anyone else, we really shouldn't be surprised if the students, and particularly the brightest ones, get the message and decide to do their own thing without limits and without regard to anyone else.

Actually, it is really only after the first world war that we in this country departed from an education with the double commitment: to character education (a phrase which draws snickers and sneers in educational groups today) as well as to provisioning and honing the mind. Since World War I, we have bit by bit withdrawn from a conscious effort to develop good citizens and sturdy human beings.

For many high-minded theorists this transition has been regarded as a purging and a purification. Recognizing that a peaceful world requires the eventual elimination of exclusive provincial value systems which make you my enemy because we disagree on what is most important in life, they have sought to produce in the academic community a model of open-mindedness. It was not so much their concern to separate each person from his own value system as to create an atmosphere where nobody passed judgment on anybody else's pattern of values. This objective was fortified by the democratic concept of the worth of each individual and by certain tenets of Christ's teachings.

The trend toward the disavowal of character education has been given further impetus by the increase in the size of many universities. An institution which serves only hundreds of students can interact with them as human beings and develop relationships wherein the teaching personnel can know and react to what the student's knowledge means to him and how he uses it. An institution which is serving tens of thousands of students is almost forced to regard the student as just a unit of intellectual raw material. To sustain any kind of character education for such a volume of students would require new techniques and new concepts and more staff and this did not turn out to be of sufficient concern to warrant that expenditure of effort and resources.

Further, the democratization of the student body has rendered any effort toward character education a very, very complex undertaking. I shall never forget an incident shortly after World War II when, as an enthusiastic and callow Dean of Students, I summoned to my office two students whom I had encountered in what I regarded as wholly inappropriate conduct for a public lounge. I was, with the greatest professional skill, masking my indignation when they entered and the girl, with patently unmasked indignation, demanded, "What's your problem?" I was so stunned, I immediately played my ace of trumps and said, "Surely, you wouldn't carry on like that in your own home." And she snapped right back, "You've got to be kidding! Of course I do."

I imagine that many a young college officer has been fortunately jolted into a recognition of the limits of his judgments as the campus has come to be populated with students of exceedingly diverse backgrounds.

And so, with a number of arguments and pressures favoring the change, a large part of the academic community has gradually abandoned any formal effort to develop in the student attitudes and behavior which will help him be a useful member of society and a competent and self-confident individual. Even the most superficial evaluation of the students in college and those recently out of college reveals a personal disorientation of serious proportions. We must remember that it is not just the dummies, but many young people of great intellectual and personal potential who are dropping out to be flower children, or turning to narcotics, or leading Quixotic assaults upon the institutions of society. No matter which of these unproductive paths they are traveling, I think we can assume they chose it because they found nothing particularly valid, challenging, and productive within the society from which they turned, and, in many cases, that society was an institution of higher learning.

If you examine the other end of the youth spectrum, the young people who are blazing trails in harmony with and as a part of society—the Peace Corpsmen, the tutors of underprivileged children, and other dedicated social servants—their activities are for the most part, self-selected, voluntary, and apart from the university experience. In those rare instances where an academic leader of broad humane vision manages to combine the formal studies in his discipline with the actual improvement of human living, the results speak for themselves. At Dartmouth College, Dean Myron Tribus has required engineering students to visit a crippled children's center and design some mechanical device to counteract one of the crippling handicaps observed at the center. What such an experience adds to engineering studies cannot be specifically identified, but it does add in a most creative way to the student's appreciation of his studies and to his own self-esteem. The point of the illustration is, of course, that this is an activity required of the student according to an educator's value judgment about student attitudes and conduct.

The university must, I believe, plan its services to its students with a view to the personal and social consequences of its decisions, making bold judgments about the curriculum and about college rules and about those public issues on which it will take an official stand and those on which it will not, according to its judgment of what will best fortify the student for the world in which he lives and what will best serve all of mankind.

Such judgments require not only great wisdom, but also deep humility and a willingness to review the judgment whenever responsible people propose the necessity to reconsider.

Any proposal for this kind of departure from the present academic orthodoxy will elicit certain predictable counter-arguments. One is the quotation from Professor Mayhew, cited earlier, that it is the appropriate business of the family and the church to govern the conduct, form the attitudes, and shape the philosophy of the young. This view strikes me as naive.

Education does have consequences. There is much to suggest that the universities in recent decades have done their work so well that the church and the family have been rendered less and less able to serve effectively in the development of character. The university's pre-eminent commitment to the open mind has been so effectively conveyed that many parents who are the product of higher education are reluctant to insist upon or even try to persuade their children of the importance of certain patterns of conduct, observing in the parent-child relationship the open-mindedness they were taught to honor.

This is not the place to try to evaluate the influence the church presently exerts upon the young. I will only observe that one possible explanation for the confusion and the declining influence of the church is that its leaders have also hearkened to the message of their alma maters, and have replaced the "Thou shalt not's" and the "Thou shalt's" with "perhapses" or "It's a matter of your own conscience" or discussion groups, or other current manifestations of open-mindedness.

Somebody is going to have to make decisions about what kind of individual conduct and what kind of group action will make society work and then try to enlist the populace in delivering those things. Certainly it would seem that academic personnel who are chosen for creative brains and who are expected to spend some time in creative thought would be one most logical source to turn to. Furthermore, the undergraduate years constitute the most critical period in attitudinal development. These are the years when there is abundant energy, when the young person has accumulated a reservoir of knowledge that he wants to put to work, when his direct responsibilities for other people are minimal and when many are most ready to respond to challenge. If the student finds no challenge meaningful to him, if he encounters in the university only a sequence of learned people each narrowly devoted to his own field of interest and apparently indifferent to the tough problems that are battering the outside world, it is no wonder that his disillusionment is great, and he rejects the generations over 30, and seeks dramatic ways to show his contempt for their society.

It is time for some specifics. I suggest there are certain value judgments, which may involve restrictions of conduct, that are appropriate and necessary for the university.

First, there are those restrictions which are necessary to the effective and orderly and creative operation of an intellectual agency. Those would include:

1. The insistence upon a respectful hearing for every person the university sees fit to invite to speak on campus. Picketing and various attempts to harass or embarrass or drown out a speaker can only lead to a reduction of academic freedom. Speakers so treated may very well stop accepting invitations, and some universities, to their abiding shame, have disinvited speakers or chosen not to invite certain speakers out of fear of student behavior.

2. The rejection of emotionalism and sensationalism as antithetical to the conduct of intellectual endeavor. The purpose of discussion is to try to increase rational understanding. In these times when our society is more and more polarized on tough public issues, the university, above all, must set an example of objectivity

and dispassion in the discovery of wiser choices and in the arrival at more just compromises, instead of permitting itself to become the arena for inflammatory and uncivilized strife.

3. The prohibition of the physical capture of university premises or university employees by college personnel.

Next are the judgments about the university's general obligations in the present context of society. These might include such items as:

1. The insistence that in every aspect of the university, there shall be no discrimination on the basis of race, color, or religion.

2. A commitment on the part of the university to observe public law and to cooperate with public authorities in maintaining public law. (The whole question of the university's tolerance or encouragement of civil disobedience needs a thorough airing, but that is another speech.)

Finally, there is the larger area of the specific purposes that an institution may elect to set for itself and the specific requirements which those purposes entail. To illustrate, let me quote the Statement of Purpose of Rockford College.

The fundamental purpose of Rockford College is to provide an educational program which will assist the student to develop the full use of his intellectual capabilities and to call into play his

highest motives so that he may be a creative, courageous and constructive member of society.

The educational program presents, through
formal studies, a broad range of theoretical knowledge, attempting to give the student an understanding of himself, of society, of the natural
universe, and of the world of art and of the
humanities. The College further includes in the
learning experience a diversified program of activities permitting the student many informal opportunities to augment, test and apply the knowledge
obtained in his studies.

The philosophy of the College is based upon
these premises:

Man is a thinking and feeling being. Therefore,
the College seeks to confirm in each student a
concern for truth, a respect for fact, the habit of
inquiry, the practice of intellectual discipline, and
the art of creative expression.

Man is a social being. Therefore, the College
nurtures in the student a belief in the inherent
dignity and worth of each individual. It seeks to
help the student discover the attitudes and conduct which will lead him to exercise that integrity
and responsibility which are vital to a free society
and provide a basis for mutual trust among persons,
communities and nations.

Man is a spiritual being. Therefore, the College
proposes to each student the importance of finding
significance in life in religious terms and the necessity of discovering a hierarchy of personal values
to which he will commit himself.

Finally, Rockford College seeks to improve and
refine the educational process so that its program
will be valid and vital for each generation of
students.

Obviously, what I have been proposing runs counter to the usual concept of academic freedom. Academic freedom is generally regarded in the university as an absolute. It is not and cannot be an absolute. There are concentric frameworks of restriction which operate on every campus, no matter how much scholars might wish otherwise. If a professor chooses to use his students in scientific experiments which are judged harmful to the physical or mental health of the students, the university must terminate the experiment. The discontinuance of the work with psychedelic drugs on the part of Professor Leary at Harvard may be an example. Dangerous experimentation must be limited, academic freedom to the contrary notwithstanding.

There is the further limit of the performance of contractual obligation. A man hired to teach astronomy who decides to use his astronomy classes to teach modern dance would have to mend his ways or his services would be terminated.

I believe most scholars would agree that there are some public laws of which violations cannot be tolerated even in the name of academic freedom.

There are the further limits that may be required in order to fulfill the duly constituted purposes of the institution. For example, I believe a church-related college has a legitimate right to confine its enrollment and/or its faculty to people who are members of its parent church. It is my understanding that such special institutional restrictions are not opposed by the

AAUP or the American Civil Liberties Union or any major accrediting agency, provided only that the college makes its special purposes and limits known to students and to professors before they decide to become a part of the institution.

It is, in my judgment, only by a painstaking determination of the purposes and priorities of each institution and by a specific and publicly proclaimed definition of them that any university can save itself from the drift and confusion and fragmentation and cross purposes which are taking an ever greater toll of time and energy and unity on the American campus. It is only by having an institution-wide agreement about objectives that a university can make legitimate and acceptable decisions about such confounding questions as should the university tolerate exclusively black organizations while prohibiting exclusively white ones. Beyond making it possible for the university just to continue operating, it is only as the university makes clear the specific nature of how it chooses to serve society that society can judge whether it is worthy of the enormous increases in funds which higher education requires year by year.

In the United States, part of the most cherished folklore has been that education was the touchstone for glory. We have had the naive assumption that all would be well if we could simply process all the people through an educational system characterized by highly trained teachers, large salaries, small classes, well-supplied libraries and laboratories, and equitable treatment for all races. The upheavals in our most respected institutions of learning, and the violently antisocial conduct of some people who are supposedly well-educated are shaking this simple faith in the educational process to a perilous degree. The old answers about academic freedom are wearing thin. The general public is beginning to perceive the truth that was stated so well in an editorial in the July, 1968, issue of *Fortune* magazine. "All order, it is true, requires limitation of freedom and results in some degree of injustice, but without order, neither freedom nor justice is possible." The public is properly beginning to require that the university not only recognize this fact of social existence, but that it teach that fact to its students.

It is only in offering this rather comprehensive view of what education ought to be and ought to do that a meaningful response to "Who Should Run the University?" can be provided.

Turning to that question, the terms trustee and regent, bespeak the assumption that education is responsible to the general public, or to the government, and that the people who bear that title are to see that the work of the educational institution they serve is in harmony with the interests of the public or the government.

With the trustee, as successively with student, faculty, and president, I wish to mention certain natural disqualifications and then the special competence they may have for participation in the major decisions of a university.

In many institutions of higher learning, a significant portion of the policy board is composed of graduates of that university. It is obviously probable that an alumnus chosen as a trustee will have a deep interest in and a significant familiarity with his alma mater and that is good. It is not so obvious that his alumnus-hood poses one important hazard in his service as a policymaker. Many successful people have the subconscious assumption that their college was quite good when they were there because they, themselves, turned out so well and consequently they may have an automatic resistance to fundamental change in the institution. There is the supposition that if the policies worked so well for me as they were, why tamper with them. For this reason, it seems advisable to seek to balance the genuine advantage of having a number of alumni trustees with an offsetting advantage of a substantial portion of trustees of other academic backgrounds. A policy board that characteristically resists innovation cannot possibly do justice to the educational process.

Another common hazard in university policy boards is that the people chosen as trustees are often executives in large enterprises. The experience and perspective and talents they provide are of great benefit, but here again their particular circumstances pose particular disadvantages. In a corportion, there is a clear hierarchy of responsibility, and if the appropriate officers agree on a new course of action, that action can and should be implemented thereupon. In a good university, each member of the ranked faculty has his own particular competence and his own legitimate basis for reacting to a given proposal for change, and major decisions affecting him which are made by remote bodies are not accepted as readily by him as by his presumed hierarchical counterpart in a corporation. A university properly needs more time and more deliberation than the corporation to alter course effectively, and the trustee of corporate background needs to remember this difference.

There are many inherent advantages of a policy board composed of people not engaged full time in the university. First, the members can bring to bear on difficult questions an objectivity which those who are party to an issue cannot. Their group judgment is not weighted by friendships and past favors and sentiment.

Second, their allegiance is to the welfare of the total institution and not to any particular limb of the academic body. In the tough conflicts between students and administration or faculty and administration, and these seem to be on the increase, an outside policy board should be better able to see beyond the issue to what is best for the university than could one of the parties to the conflict.

The other trustee qualification I wish to mention is the one most pertinent to the heart of this statement. Drawn from the larger community and, hopefully, representative of the best brains and most dedicated citizens of the larger community, the trustees should be better suited than other constituencies of the university to make the ultimate judgments about the objectives of the institution, about how that institution is to serve society, and about the fundamental policies which will most effectively deliver those objectives and that service.

If higher education has gotten off the track, if it has redirected its principal effort from serving students to the production of new knowledge, if it is contributing to an amoral and a demoralized society, then the blame must be shared, but the greatest portion of blame belongs to the trustees who have the final responsibility for what the institution is and what it does. There is the clear impression that many boards of trustees have either by choice, or by skillful administrative persuasion, tended to direct their deliberations and their energies primarily to finances, to the acquisition, the safeguarding and the allocation of money. This may be the field of university activity in which some trustees have the greatest competence, but that is no excuse for default in their obligations. If the trustees are not wholly cognizant of the scope and the consequences of the work of their university, and if these are not in keeping with their collective judgment about what that work ought to be for the benefit of society, then the trustees are delinquent in the trust which they have accepted. The major thrust of trustee endeavors should be to determine in broad outline what the university should be doing and to establish and refine policies which will enable the university to do those things effectively.

As for the student, there is little that is persuasive in behalf of granting to the student authority in making university decisions.

Somehow, the spokesmen for student power seem to have forgotten that there is an apprenticeship function on the way to competence in any complex endeavor, particularly in the making of judgments for a human institution. Jacques Barzun observes, "The truth is that to speak of democracy in an institution set up to give technical services, such as a school or hospital, is to misuse language and think like a child. Not even in the agencies of a democratic government is there direct democracy: the citizen in the post office does not participate in fixing the price of stamps or promoting the clerks."

The students do have important counsel to give. Their evaluation of individual courses and professors and the curriculum needs to be solicited and taken into account by those who do make the decisions. We also must acknowledge that students bring fresh perspective and energy and imagination and they constitute a fertile source of new projects and new ways of doing things. Student advice and suggestions and criticism need to be solicited and given serious attention, but cannot be the sole basis for judgment.

If the objective phrased by Mr. Bundy and the 7,500 educators interrogated by the Office of Education is to persist, if the academic freedom of the faculty is the university's first objective, then the faculty should indeed run the university and the president and the administrative staff should be the agents of the faculty, delivering the equipment and services needed by the professors to carry on their work.

I am strongly convinced that the primary mission should be something rather different. Furthermore, I would quote to those professors who think the faculty should be the university decision maker, James Thurber's line, "He who would avoid life's wriest laughter should not attain the thing he's after."

A good university faculty is about the most inherently fragmented body ever devised by man. Each faculty member has his own specialty with its deep-vested interests. To a significant degree, each man is in opposition to all the rest. In such matters as budget allocations, space assignments, equipment, leaves of absence, secretarial staff, fellowship allotments, library purchases, curriculum change, and redistribution of required courses and many other important matters, it is every man for himself. The jockeying for position and the political in-fighting among faculty members which characterizes many campuses does not, I think, arise because the teaching creature is congenitally cantankerous, but because the order of academic things places the faculty member in an eternally and critically competitive situation. Major decisions of an entire faculty are slow and agonizing and too often reflect the current balance of political power on campus rather than the objective collective judgment of the individuals.

To suppose that such an agency could accomplish the numerous, complex and varied important decisions of a university is not realistic.

Furthermore, an able faculty member is almost by definition a specialist. He sees the world through his own specialist's telescope. You've heard of the statistician who drowned in a river that had an average depth of two and one-half feet. If the astronomers and the bio-chemists and the Sanskrit scholars ever had to wade through the preparation of the total budget, which is a significant part of running a university, they might not drown in it, but there might be some casualties by slashing of wrists.

The faculty does have unique and essential competence for running a large part of the university, and if they are not given the power to make the decisions in their areas of competence, it will not be a university for long. Once the objectives of the university are clearly identified, it is the faculty that must develop the curriculum to meet those objectives, establish and maintain the standards of academic performance, propose and implement educational innovation, and be generally responsible for teaching and research activities.

Beyond those responsibilities, the faculty must be called upon for advice and sometimes participation in decisions affecting student life, relationships with the community, the government and the general public, long-range planning, and many other matters.

Finally, the president. As a preliminary to my comments on this officer, I would like to repeat an observation Buckminster Fuller has made. In the system of American education, the brightest minds are identified by college faculties and are encouraged, coaxed, or lured into graduate school in one discipline or another where they are trained to be specialists. This leaves the students of moderate ability and the dunderheads to be the generalists who become college presidents, corporate executives, and government leaders. I fear there may be as much truth as humor in this mordant remark, and if there is, it provides a grievous obstacle for the recommendations presented in this paper. For it is my judgment that it must be the president who runs the university. I believe it is essential that the man who holds that office be a highly capable scholar whose particular academic capacity is as a comprehensivist. But before elaborating on what ought to be the talents of the president, it is useful to register upon present circumstances and how they have skewed the work and the concept of the university president.

The enormous variety of federal programs for higher education, and the enormous volume of federal funds that flows to the campus, and the dependence of the university upon those funds make it desirable that the head of any major university have, as one of his principal qualifications, a wealth of contacts in Washington and a reputation which will earn him appointments to the Board of the National Science Foundation, Presidential Task Forces, or other posts of distinction and visibility within the government. Furthermore, the professional organizations such as the American Council on Education and the Association of American Colleges have taken on a critical role in the development of federal funding policy and the lobbying in behalf of federal grant legislation and the university needs to protect its own position through these agencies. Thus the selection of the university executive is influenced by the Washington track record of the candidate and the level of off-campus commitments which he holds and to which he is likely to be named.

Another present circumstance which tends to skew the office and the activity of the university president is a high level of factionalism within the campus constituencies. The consequences are to be noted in the rejoicing of several universities recently in the appointment of new chief executives noted for their talents in mediation.

There are numerous pressures and demands in higher education today which not only direct the time and the energy of the president away from the genuine business of academic statesmanship, but which seem to be changing the concept of the presidential office from that of educational philosopher to that of professional manager. This is, I believe, a vicious circle. The less time the president devotes directly to the educational mission of his own institution, the more the problems multiply which demand his time on other matters.

The primary and consuming work of the university president should be as first scholar of the faculty, doing his creative work in understanding how his university can best serve mankind, in analyzing and anticipating the changes in society so that the educational services will be dealing with what is and will be, rather than what was.

The president also has heavy teaching assignments. It is his continual responsibility to teach his colleagues in the faculty, student body, and administration the concepts that underlie university policy and think through with those colleagues how their large decisions relate to those policies and how they can best be implemented. He also bears a critically important teaching task in his relationship to the trustees. If their decisions are to strengthen the university, then he must have helped them to understand what is at issue.

It may be that some university presidents suppose that they should not only be the principal agent between trustees and campus personnel, but should also be a buffer to keep the two groups as far apart as possible and filter out those thoughts and comments from the one side that would be abrasive to the other. On the contrary, I think the president has an obligation to inform the trustees fully and candidly of the whole range of complications with which he must deal. To his trustee "classes" he should bring "guest speakers" from the student body and faculty who can articulate the differing views on the issues before the board. The continuing education of the trustees is in the hands of the president.

The president also is the teacher of the general public. It is he who must explain what the university is doing, why it is valid, why it is important, and why the services provided by his institution deserve ever-increasing financial support. He must not only be clear and persuasive on the theory of his university but must be armed with illustrations from the classroom and laboratory and student programs to support his case.

I wish to suggest that present difficulties and dilemmas faced by universities may, in large part, be the result of the transition from the philosopher-president to the campus-troubleshooter-and-all-purpose-advisor-and-distinguished-director-of-distant-enterprises president.

A previous generation of university executives foresaw the disadvantages of federal aid for education and analyzed with prophetic accuracy the outcome of federal subsidy in the letters they wrote to Congressman Barden in the late 1940s. So persuasive were their arguments that their position prevailed, and President Truman's enthusiastic thrust for federal aid to education failed to pass in Congress. But, 20 years later after many federal aid bills were passed unopposed by university executives, the distinguished president of the Carnegie Corporation predicted in his 1967 address to the Association of American Colleges that private education as we have known it may well disappear. When the federal government is paying everybody's bills, private is no longer private.

The most difficult financial bind faced by the university is meeting the high cost of the tremendous volume of research. The research function has been inflated and inflated and inflated by an enormous outpouring of federal funds, which has now reached the point that the university could not possibly sustain the quantity of research from its own traditional financial sources. And so, having become altogether dependent upon federal funds, when the Congress suddenly reverses political course and cuts $5 billion out of the expenditures, universities from coast to coast suddenly find themselves in a huge financial mess. It is impossible to be dependent and independent concurrently. Dependence upon federal funds is just that, dependence.

I predict that if our nation remains solvent, and if our universities are to retain or regain control of their own destinies, it will only be as a result of a dramatic change in the concept of federal funding of research. In the new order, the federal government would continue to support only that university research which is

determined by the government to be necessary for purposes of the government, such as research into defense,
public health, or public finance, and the government
would pay the full cost of that research, including
overhead *and* a fair profit. All the other academic
research would be limited to that for which the university can find an industrial or foundation sponsor,
or which it can undertake out of its own general
resources.

The other deep and grievous difficulties faced by
universities, the disruptions and take-overs and in-fighting, are, like the financial peril, the result of a failure
of presidential leadership to hold high before the academic community the purposes of its existence and
insist upon action appropriate to these purposes.

At this point, I wish to present a quotation from
Walter Lippmann.

> For modern men are living today amidst the
> consequences of emancipation from established
> authority. The dream of Franklin and Jefferson,
> as Mr. James A. Perkins describes it, was of "an
> open society, free of both ecclesiastical and civil
> control, with little to fear from the uninhibited
> search for truth and for experiments in the appli-
> cation of truth." The preponderant majority of
> our people in America today have arrived at such
> an open society. They have found, I submit to
> you, that as they are emancipated from established
> authority they are not successfully equipped to
> deal with the problems of American society and of
> their private lives. They are left with the feeling

that there is a vacuum within them, a vacuum where there were the signs and guide posts of an ancestral order, where there used to be ecclesiastical and civil authority, where there was certainly, custom, usage and social status, a fixed way of life. One of the great phenomena of the human condition in the modern age is the dissolution of the ancestral order, the erosion of established authority, having lost the light and the leading, the guidance and the support, the discipline that the ancestral order provided, modern men are haunted by a feeling of being lost and adrift, without purpose and meaning in the conduct of their lives.

The thesis which I am putting to you is that the modern void, which results from the vast and intricate process of emancipation and rationalization, must be filled, and that the universities must fill the void because they alone can fill it.

It is a high destiny. But it must be accepted and it must be realized.[1]

It is a difficult thing to admit error. One wonders whether those now running our universities will have the courage to face up to what must be done, even when the university is so evidently threatened by the consequences of its erroneous past theories. One wonders whether the academic community will be able to bring itself to ban student organizations committed to the use of violence and take the other actions that are necessary to restore the university to the conditions in which learning can take place and students can be helped to become creative, courageous, and constructive members of society. If order is restored and appropriate unifying principles reasserted, it will only come about because an enlightened president is running his university.

No committee or group can make the judgments which are required every day to keep a university running. No committee or group can keep itself sufficiently informed about the interactions and frictions among university personnel or be familiar enough with the relative importance of their requests to know when to say, "Yes," and when to say, "No," and when to ask for more information in order to keep the whole system working together. And no committee can maintain the consistency of decisions which has to prevail in a human agency.

To summarize, it is the president who must run the university. He is subordinate to the trustees and must work within the limits and toward the objectives they prescribe. But, if he is a competent president, their prescriptions will most often be what he has recommended.

To the faculty will be delegated that authority which is properly theirs. The president will do his utmost to support them in their work according to their judgments, but when their actions conflict with university policy, or when faculty interests are at odds with the interests of students, or security guards, or other university personnel, it is the president who is the last echelon of mediation or judgment.

In running the university, the president's pre-eminent roles are as theorist, interpreter, implementer and judge of the purposes of the institution.

SECOND LECTURE

H. BRUCE FRANKLIN

The question Who should run the universities? is not academic, for American universities are not academies. They are essential sources of power within our society, and thus throughout the world. The battles to control them will widen and become more fierce in the next several years and decades. The universities are not even independent entities, for they need huge and growing amounts of capital, and both their tools and their products are highly socialized and interdependent. Our question is not academic but historic.

Presumably none of us is here to deal in utopian speculation. If we were, we could consider the verb "should" in all its dimensions, trying to find some proper hypothetical mixture of justice, legitimacy, efficiency, creativity, and so on. We could then run down some of the following propositions, among others:

The rich should run the universities because only they have the political and economic power to do so.

The poor should run the universities because they have the greatest needs for educational and research facilities.

Faculties should run the universities because they are so intelligent and creative.

Students should run the universities because they have the most at stake.

The Department of Defense should run the universities because of the threat of communism and national liberation movements.

Administrators should run the universities because they are disinterested professionals, standing above the sordid struggle of the other groups.

I suppose that when President Howard and I were chosen to be antagonists in this rational debate, it was tacitly assumed that he would argue for the power of administrators and I would proclaim all power to the students and faculty. I haven't as yet read his lecture, but I wish to make it clear that I believe the slogans "Student Power" and "Faculty Power" to be increasingly misleading. These existing groups—administration, faculty, and students—are not the actual protagonists in the struggle. These groups—a more accurate word would be groupings—represent a kind of false consciousness; and they fracture under the impact of events, revealing the real struggle behind these forms —class struggle.

In order to understand how this struggle takes place in this arena, and why it does at this particular time, we have to understand the historical development of the modern American university, who now actually controls it, the class character of both its faculty and its student body, how all these interrelate with each other and with the rest of society, and how they are all rapidly shifting.

I would like to distinguish three stages in the history of the university; the medieval or feudal university; the university of the bourgeoisie; and the future university of the working people. Each of the first two stages has contained the preconditions of the emerging subsequent stage. That is, what we are now witnessing is an institution in the process of transcending itself, being revolutionized, turning into its opposite at the very moment it is developing to its own extreme.

In the medieval university, student and faculty power was total and devotion to the humanities was complete. It was a feudal institution, unequivocally servicing the church and the aristocracy. The medieval university bequeathed to its successor a legacy at once rich and reactionary, precious and dangerous. The ideal of contemplation outside the struggle of society; the fraternity of scholars; the quest for philosophic, as opposed to practical, truth; the purity of the academy —all these are still present to some degree in the university. And, strange as it may seem, the university is the last stronghold of that central medieval concept —so completely shattered by the Renaissance, the rise of capitalism, and modern science—the ideal of timelessness. The medieval university still exists in the minds of many academics, who occasionally resent the intrusions of the war machine almost as much as they

resent the protest demonstrations against it. Periodi-
cally, from Cardinal Newman's 1852 glorification of
a dead institution, "The Idea of the University," to
S. I. Hayakawa's recent wistful claim that "in another
time I would have been a priest,"[1] that ideal is resur-
rected to serve as a shield against the dynamic forces
reshaping a far different university.

The university of the bourgeoisie has itself developed
stage by stage. In America, the colonial university—
most typically Harvard and Yale—on the surface seems
to have been the most advanced form of the medieval
university. Totally under the control of the New
England theocracy, and totally committed to an orthodox religious view of experience, it would seem the
bastion of conservatism. But its religious orthodoxy
was Puritanism, American Puritanism at that, and just
as American Puritanism provided an ideological base
for the rising merchant class, the colonial university,
only superficially transformed, became a main base of
political and economic power for that class.

In Europe, the demands of dynamically developing
nineteenth century capitalism brought a radical innovation to the idea of the university, the German model,
stressing scientific research, scientific method in all
fields, and graduate instruction. This model reached
America at a crucial time, shortly after the Land Grant
Act of 1862 and the radical changes in class relations
brought about by the Civil War, and during the powerful westward expansion of youthful American capital-

ism. The land grant university, rather than the New England college, was to be the prototype of the university of the future, though that was to include the graduate and research faculties imported by Johns Hopkins University.

The next qualitative changes came with the depression and World War II, when the federal government became increasingly involved in the universities; this represented part of the process of the collapse of private enterprise capitalism and its replacement by monopoly and state capitalism. In World War II the university was recruited directly into war research, and the cold war, together with the increasing demands of monopoly capitalism at home and abroad, has fused what is now commonly called the military-industrial-educational complex, which may be understood as an early stage of state capitalism.

In this stage the medieval university, a cosmos fused by a single purpose, has become completely transformed into its opposite, what Clark Kerr has aptly named the multiversity, where the central value is the bourgeois ethic of competition. Competition reigns supreme at all levels and in all activities. The community of scholars has been replaced by the academic marketplace; grades and class standings determine the course of life, and, for many young men, whether they will live at all; departments and schools are pitted against each other; the faculty, student body, administration,

and board of trustees struggle against each other and
against their counterparts in other universities; the
competitiveness of football teams, fraternities, and
departmental hiring committees is only an outward
manifestation of the battles for money relentlessly
waged in, through, and by every segment of the multiversity structure. For, as Clark Kerr has put it, the
multiversity is "a mechanism held together by administrative rules and powered by money." [2]

To illustrate the archetypal multiversity, Kerr offered
this description of his own (this was in 1963) University of California:

> The University of California last year had oper-
> ating expenditures from all sources of nearly half a
> billion dollars, with almost another 100 million for
> construction; a total employment of over 40,000
> people, more than IBM and in a far greater variety
> of endeavors; operations in over a hundred loca-
> tions, counting campuses, experiment stations,
> agricultural and urban extension centers, and
> projects abroad involving more than fifty coun-
> tries; nearly 10,000 courses in its catalogues; some
> form of contact with nearly every industry, nearly
> every level of government, nearly every person in
> its region. Vast amounts of expensive equipment
> were serviced and maintained. Over 4,000 babies
> were born in its hospitals. It is the world's largest
> purveyor of white mice. It will soon have the
> world's largest primate colony. It will soon also
> have 100,000 students—30,000 of them at the
> graduate level; yet much less than one third of its
> expenditures are directly related to teaching. It

already has nearly 200,000 students in extension courses—including one out of every three lawyers and one out of every six doctors in the state.[3]

This multiversity, comparable to a small nation, is only one of the giants, even within California. Surely nobody would argue with Kerr's contention that the multiversity "has become a prime instrument of national purpose." [4] And when we realize that "six universities received 57% of federal research funds in a recent year, and twenty universities received 79%," that the knowledge industry as a whole constitutes 29 percent of the gross national product and is growing at a rate twice that of the rest of the economy,[5] when we realize all this, we must recognize that the slogans "Student Power" and "Faculty Power" are, to say the least, inadequate. The only adequate slogan for control over an institution this central to our society is "Power to the people."

The multiversity is at one and the same time the highest form of the university of the bourgeoisie and the developing form of the university of the masses of the people. Like the other economic institutions of overdeveloped capitalist society, it is in the process of shifting from control by private enterprise through control by monopoly capital to control by the state. Though this state calls itself a public state, it is in fact an instrument of monopoly capital, safely under the control of the corporate rich. Its internal contradictions, however, do indeed prepare the way for a true government of the people. The multiversity presents the contradictions of this stage of development in striking form. Of all the major institutions in the society, it perpetuates the most frankly elitist values; yet it does so behind a totally egalitarian facade. It is the wellspring of articulate bourgeois liberalism and the seedbed of the most outspoken radicalism. Its virtually all-white and overwhelmingly male faculties profess the most democratic of bourgeois ideals to a student body now one-third female, becoming racially mixed, and rapidly widening in class origin. It is an essential bulwark of the status quo and a source of fundamental social, economic, and political changes. And the question Who should run the universities? is seriously debated at a time when it should be perfectly clear that no group can control the universities without controlling society as a whole.

Who now actually does run the universities? As far as ultimate power, the answer is very simple: the owning class runs the universities, much as they run the rest of society.

In capitalist society, power comes from ownership, and ownership comes from power. The owning class not only owns the means of production but also the means of communication. All major political candidates must therefore either themselves be members of the ruling class or be directly selected by it.

One must understand this power historically. When commodities were typically produced by a man who both owned the tools and did the labor, there was no question as to who did or should own the product. The great historical question Who should own the product? arose when one man owned the tools and another did the work. That question was neither posed nor answered in abstract ethical debate; it was merely answered by power: because there were more workers and fewer tools than were needed, the man who owned the tools had the *power* to claim sole ownership of the product. This is, of course, the central premise of capitalist society. Its consequences are obviously cumulative: the more one owns, the more power one has; the more power one has, the more one can own. Two of the central ethics that follow from this are: the person who does own something is the person who should own it; those who have power are the ones who should have it.

Now of course there are antitheses to all this. The actual work of capitalist society is not done by the owning class, and the working class knows this, dimly in prosperous times, acutely in periods of economic stress. Work, as well as ownership, is at least a potential source of power, and the working class recognizes this in practice: its main effective tactic is withdrawing its labor. By challenging the legitimacy of the power of the owning class, the working class makes possible a challenge of the source of that power—private property.

In the university, useful labor is performed by students, faculty, administrators, and non-teaching workers, both blue- and white-collar. Some of the tools are physical, such as books, classroom buildings, equipment, etc.; these are made by the interdependent labor of intellectuals and industrial workers, both directly and by using capital created by other workers. The main tool and the main product is knowledge, which in its totality is nothing less than the most important product of all previous humanity. There are at least three distinct kinds of knowledge used and produced in the university. First is useful knowledge or "know how," which creates, among other things, factories, industries, power, and empires. This kind of knowledge can be owned, at least temporarily, a fact attested to by the patent office, by the laws governing ownership of industrial research, and by the security classifications of the Department of Defense. The other two kinds may be called ideological knowledge and cultural knowledge; these belong to the class that produced them and serve the interests of that class. Ultimate power and legal control over all the physical tools and products of the university lie in the hands of the corporate elite, both directly, through their total occupation of the boards of trustees and regents, and indirectly, through the political apparatus they control. The same is true for the useful knowledge, which becomes the property of either corporations or the state. And by having ultimate control over the procedures and principles of hiring, the trustees and regents so far have been able to make sure that only the culture and ideology of their own class and of previous ruling classes can be propagated in their universities.

The lines of power in the so-called private universities are neatly drawn. Stanford and Columbia are good examples because research on the power structure of each has been both thorough and conveniently assembled.[6]

All power at Stanford legally derives from Leland Stanford's plunder through Mrs. Stanford's will. It legally belongs to the board of trustees, which can be broken down into four interrelated groupings: San Francisco finance and construction, oil, electronics, and aerospace (it includes the presidents of General Dynamics, of Hewlett-Packard, and of Northrop Corporation). The main business of Stanford University is maintaining and expanding an economic empire in the Pacific basin, that is, the areas of the world contiguous to the Pacific Ocean. It does this by producing the needed research, ideology, hardware, and super-skilled manpower, and by providing a vehicle for the interlocking of the appropriate corporate giants. The overall theory of this Pacific basin empire is itself a Stanford product. Together with Stanford Research Institute, a wholly-owned subsidiary, Stanford is the nation's second largest university contractor with the Department of Defense. The selection of Trustee David Packard to be deputy secretary of defense will undoubtedly improve this position, as will the presidency of Kenneth Pitzer who unites in his own person oil (Tenneco), aerospace (NASA), and construction (Brown and Root). The overall purpose of Stanford research was well defined back in 1951 by Stanford Research Institute's director, Jesse Hobson:

> This nation occupies 6 percent of the land area of the world, has 7 percent of the world's population, but it now produces 50 percent of the world's goods and possesses 67 percent of the world's wealth.
>
> Research must be the heart, the foundation, the life blood of our present defense economy if we are to maintain this position.[7]

Stanford is the proud home of Professor Eugene Staley's strategic hamlet plan for Vietnam, as well as the ill-fated McNamara Line, whose sophisticated electronic components were to be produced by firms represented on the board of trustees—Hewlett-Packard, Watkins-Johnson, General Telephone and Telegraph. The School of Engineering and the School of Business are integrated directly with the Stanford Industrial Park. The Electrical Engineering Department, which provided the provost while aerospace and electronics were ousting the railroads and shipping from domination of the board, has more faculty members than the departments of history, classics, anthropology, and philosophy combined. The Hoover Institution on War, Revolution and Peace, which has open connections with the FBI and CIA, is one of the world's main centers of cold war propaganda. It was founded explicity "to demonstrate the evils of the doctrines of Karl Marx . . . thus to protect the American way of life"; according to the *Wall Street Journal* (June 2, 1967), it now has "a network of agents around the world." [8] The board of trustees has direct and interlocked financial interests in Thailand, Vietnam, Laos, Indonesia, Malaysia, the Philippines, Australia, Peru, Bolivia, Chile, Venezuela, Guatemala, Nicaragua, Panama, Mexico, Korea, Taiwan, and Japan; in the latter two Stanford has graduate campuses. Stanford is doing research on counterinsurgency in 12 of these countries. Yet when faced with a nonviolent demonstration against CIA recruiting on campus, the administration and much of the liberal faculty hold up the medieval image of the university as a sacrosanct place of tranquil and disinterested contemplation of timeless truth.

Columbia is a strikingly similar institution, whose power structure has been comprehensively analyzed in *Who Rules Columbia?* I shall not try to summarize this research, but merely point out a few of its more interesting disclosures about the board of trustees.

The mass media have heavy representation on the board, including top officers of the Columbia Broadcasting System, *The New York Times,* and the Whitney communications empire of television, radio, and publishing. Columbia's own huge real estate holdings have been involved in apparent conflict-of-interest transactions with the real estate and construction

empire of Uris Buildings Corporation, which has four
representatives on the board; the man who would be
involved in investigating such conflicts of interest,
District Attorney Frank S. Hogan, is also on the board.
The usual giant international corporations are represented not only by some of their own officers but also
by officers of CIA front organizations: ex-president
Kirk, like ex-president Sterling of Stanford, played a
crucial role in the Asia Foundation, which was both
founded and funded by the CIA; altogether at least
six trustees are prominent in organizations secretly
funded by the CIA.

Who Rules Columbia? tightly documents just how
the physical and educational resources of the university
have been consistently used to serve the material interests of its rulers. For those who would like to see
this documentation, I have brought along a few copies.

In the case of the private universities, the usual
argument employed to justify the fact that only the
wealthiest and most powerful can sit on the board of
trustees is that only they can financially support the
university. With over half of the large "private"
university's financing coming from public funds, this
argument may be somewhat open to question, even on
its own terms (forgetting the larger question as to
whether they *should* be controlling higher education
simply because they are rich and powerful). But in
the case of public universities, even this argument falls
on its face. If the people as a whole pay for the public

university, and if the presumed purpose of this university is to provide higher education and research for the people as a whole, and if, as Clark Kerr says of the University of California, it has "contact with . . . nearly every person in its region," then surely all social the University of California, it has "contact with . . . on its controlling board. But the board of regents of the typical public university is made up of precisely the same sort of person who sits on the private boards —the most powerful owners and executives of monopoly capital. The only substantive difference is that usually some politicians who belong to that same social class sit with them.

The University of California Board of Regents has eight ex-officio political members, and 16 members appointed by the governor for 16-year terms (which are, because of the advanced age of the average appointee, in effect lifetime appointments). Every one of the present 16 appointed members directly represents the state's large corporate interests. There is no representative of labor, organized or unorganized. There are no blacks, who constitute 10 percent of the state's population, or Chicanos, who constitute between 15 percent and 20 percent. The closest resemblances to academic appointees are two of Governor Reagan's latest, both from the Stanford complex: Dean Watkins, once an electrical engineering professor at Stanford, now president of Watkins-Johnson Corporation and a trustee at Stanford; and W. Glenn Campbell, director of the Hoover Institution.

Like Columbia's board, this one includes heavy representation from the corporations controlling the mass media, notably the Hearst publishing empire and the Times-Mirror Company. This board includes the major groupings found at Stanford: finance and construction, oil, aerospace, and electronics. But a very important addition is California's agro-business,[9] represented chiefly by Hunt Foods and Industries and several real estate holding corporations. California is the country's largest agricultural producer, and the University of California is intimately involved with all aspects of the state's agriculture. The board of regents consistently allocates the university's resources, that is, the people's money, to increase the profitability of the large farms, but the only efforts made to help the people who do the labor on these farms come from the campus radicals, taking the form of direct action, either in the local supermarket, in the university cafeteria, or among the farm-workers themselves. In fact during the Delano strike, now in its third year, the University of California's Extension Service extends help to the struck ranchers. The role of the board is best displayed by Allan Grant, an ex-officio member, as Reagan's appointee to head the State Board of Agriculture:

Grant is a member of the National Right to Work Committee; he has stated publicly that his farm workers come to talk to him at the back door on his 2,000 acre Visalia ranch, and he would feel he had failed in his Christian duty if they should tell him they wanted a union.[10]

The University of California Board of Regents conducts almost all its business in secret executive sessions, contrary to a basic principal of state law and to its own bylaws. It goes along with the academic freedom of all those who do not effectively challenge capitalism, but it sponsors loyalty oaths for its professors, tries to prevent spokesmen for the opposition, such as Eldridge Cleaver, from lecturing in their university, and whenever possible limits the rights of speech and assembly of the students.

California has another huge public university, the State College system, which has recently, and for good reason, been making more news than the University of California. The reason is that its student body is drawn much more from the working class, because its entrance requirements are, in bourgeois terms, "lower." The State College has its own board of trustees, which is infinitely more democratic and representative than the university's board of regents. That is, it actually includes one man who is both black and, as a union leader, supposedly a representative of working people. But this sole exception to white ruling-class rule, Edward O. Lee, has been systematically excluded from the board's deliberations on the crisis at San Francisco State.[11]

It has been argued that merely sitting on the governing board of a university does not necessarily equal having effective control over it. Those who make this argument point to the power within the universities that the faculty has, through its own senate, on tripartite committees, and within departments, over hiring and firing procedures, course content, academic regulations, etc. If it is true that the governing boards do not have the real power, one wonders why the representatives of monopoly capital fight so hard and so successfully to maintain their complete domination of these boards.[12]

The answer is simple: the oligopoly interests who constitute the boards of trustees and regents make the fundamental decisions from which all day-to-day decisions flow. By having ultimate control over hiring, they have effective self-perpetuating control. If you doubt this, imagine SDS and the Black Panther Party appointing a university faculty; it would make no effective difference whether the original organizations or their chosen faculty were to be in charge of subsequent hiring and other decisions. The trustees and regents decide how resources will be allocated, what new schools or institutes will be created, what will be the relative size and strength of the existing schools and institutes. At Stanford, even departmental control of its own finances is actually used as a means of control over the department. The administration, acting as the agent of the trustees, says, to each department,

"Here, fellows, is your pie for next year. Divide it up
any way you want." What this means, of course, is
that if one professor gets a raise, it must come either
out of the pocket of one of his colleagues or out of
his department's academic or research program. Totally
beyond question is the new business school building,
the new athletic pavilion, the doubling of the facilities
of the Hoover Institution or the quadrupling of those
of the Stanford Research Institute. The concrete evidence of real faculty impotence stands revealed in a
single fact: the detailed university budget is a closely-
guarded secret from everyone but the board of trustees
and a handful of top administrators. No one else is
even allowed to know the relative allocation of resources, much less have anything to do with deter-
mining it.

The agents of the trustees' and regents' power are
the administrations of the various universities. Of
course their role is a good deal more complicated than
that. University administrators are rather Janus-headed
figures, with one face that looks like a corporate
industrial manager and another that resembles the pure
academician.

In the most typical nineteenth century industrial
enterprises, there was no question who ran the show.
The owner was the boss. He either ran things directly
or hired managers to transmit his directives. As we
all know, that typical enterprise evolved into a joint-
stock company, then into a huge complex corporation,

and now into a labyrinthine structure of many corporations, interlocked with each other and with the
state. The corporate conglomerate is, like the multiversity, a characteristic form of the military-industrial-
educational complex of developing state capitalism. As
this evolution has taken place, the role of owner and
the role of manager have become redefined. The
managerial function has gained increasingly independent power, while, at the same time, it has become
increasingly dependent on complicated objective conditions. It is not the owner who tells the manager what
to do; both of them take their orders from the internal
dynamics of the bureaucratic and mechanical labyrinths
they "run." And although some large and important
decisions are still made by the owners, the day-to-day
operating decisions are made by the managers. Does
this group constitute, as some have argued, a distinct
new class, the managerial class, having fundamental
contradictions with the owning class? Clearly this is
not so in corporations, where the big managers get to
be, as a condition of their employment, part owners.
In the university, this does not totally apply. Is there
then a class distinction—and therefore a fundamental
contradiction—between the administration and the
board of regents or trustees? I think not. First of all,
though the administration runs the university in the
sense of managing or administering it, that is, making
the day-to-day operating decisions, it is thereby implementing purposes over which it has no control. In

practice the administration cannot question the premises of the multiversity, and to do so would be—quite literally—unthinkable for most administrators. They draw their identity, like the salary, from the class they serve and into which they merge. They are not merely the surrogates of the owning class, for as nineteenth century private enterprise capitalism evolves through corporate capitalism into state capitalism, the owning class as such becomes superfluous. Managing increasingly becomes the effective equivalent of owning and finally substitutes for it.

No contradiction between present managers or administrators and owners or trustees is a class contradiction, any more than contradictions between the management of Ford and General Motors are class contradictions, or, for that matter, any more than contradictions between the state capitalist managers of the Soviet Union and those of the United States are class contradictions. The class enemies of all these are their own working class and the peoples of the Third World. This is why the administrators of the American multiversity are as eager as their boards of trustees and regents to throw the full might of their institutions against the forces of what they call instability in the world and at home.

But the administration has limits placed upon it from other directions. Caught between the trustees or regents and the forces in rebellion against that very class, it often finds itself in the position of attempted

mediator or buffer in class struggle. This is complicated by the fact that most administrators have their
immediate origin in the faculty, a group itself torn
by internal contradictions.

The faculty of the multiversity includes powerful
businessmen, professional military officers, would-be
medieval humanist scholars, scientists with independent
contracts and dependent research teams, doctors, lawyers, and bohemian writers. According to some New
Left theorists, the faculty belongs to the "new working
class," but surely this might be true of only parts of
the faculty, relatively small parts at the so-called "top"
universities. Even those that do belong to the working
class represent one of its most privileged and highest
paid strata, and the other end of the spectrum shades
off into the managerial and owning class, particularly
in the schools of engineering and business. The salaries
of professors are directly proportional to their contribution to production, to profit, and to the ideological
and material defense of monopoly capitalism. But even
professors of the humanities are now well paid in
comparison to most of the working class; in the San
Francisco Bay Area, in fact, their starting salary is
almost as high as that of a policeman. (After doing
my graduate work and teaching at Stanford for five
years, my own take-home pay equalled what it had
been as a lieutenant in the Air Force.) Extremely few
faculty members at the prestige universities consider
themselves members of the working class, but in the

state colleges and junior colleges there is often a substantial minority who do so identify themselves, as
evidenced by the rapid growth of trade unions among
them.

Most professors, however, are both objectively and
subjectively members of the middle and petty bourgeoisie. As such, they share a very common idea of
their class—that class struggle, if it exists at all, involves
other people and springs from their irrationality. Hence
the liberal idea that conflict comes from people not
communicating well enough. As a sub-class, professors fervently cling to the belief that they, perhaps
alone of all groups, are above that sordid field of confused struggle. This belief justifies their very reason for
existence, for they believe that they alone can offer a
neutral, objective, classless, more or less *truth*ful view
of the other classes, of the history of their struggles,
and of the culture which springs from this history and
gives it comprehensible form. Their pursuit of such
pure truth incidentally commits them to lives where
they associate only with other members of the middle
and petty bourgeoisie, particularly other "professional"
people. Though they may advocate integrated schools
and housing, they live in all-white ghettoes and send
their children to tokenly integrated schools. Though
they may be sympathetic to workers in the abstract,
they probably do not know a single blue-collar worker
personally, and therefore lament that the industrial
working class is "content with their car and TV sets."

Only inside the university do the professors act on what they understand as class relationships, their relationships to the students and, sometimes, to the administration. Toward the upper level of the internal university hierarchy, professors are in a somewhat ambiguous position. There is a good deal of mobility from the faculty into the administration. In many universities administrative *labor* is spread out among the faculty. Professors do not generally question the premises of the university, and therefore do not often object to having little or no say about fundamental decisions. There is commonly a simmering resentment against administrative control over salaries, but the faculty gets more upset with the administration when it permits their security and privileges to be exposed to the onslaught of the unwashed masses, the students. For one thing all faculty members have in common, whether they sit in the highest councils of Washington or whether they are struggling humanist scholars straight out of graduate school: they have more direct power over more people's lives than exists almost anywhere in our society, with the possible exception of the military. Jerry Farber, who teaches at California State College, Los Angeles, has described this relationship in his aptly-titled essay, "Students are Niggers":

> A student . . . is expected to know his place. He calls a faculty member "Sir" or "Doctor" or "Professor"—and he smiles and shuffles as he stands outside the professor's office waiting for permis-

sion to enter. The faculty tell him what courses
to take . . .; they tell him what to read, what to
write, and, frequently, where to set the margins
on his typewriter. They tell him what's true and
what isn't. . . . The saddest cases among both black
slaves and student slaves are the ones who have so
thoroughly introjected their masters' values that
their anger is turned inward.[13]

Farber says that if he takes students into the faculty
dining room, his "colleagues get uncomfortable, as
though there were a bad smell." At the Stanford
Faculty Club, there is an exception to this, because
my colleagues seem comfortable when their students
are there as their waiters. In many buildings at Stanford, like at Cal State, the rest rooms are marked
"Faculty only."

With one foot in the working class and the other
rubbing against the ankles of the ruling class, ambig-
uously under administrative rule and clearly ruling
the students, completely dependent on the system but
often outraged by what the system does, the faculty
behaves as might be expected—it vacillates in its loyalties but in a crisis tends to line up with the party of
order. All this so far is really nothing new, and the
faculty of the multiversity as a whole tends to behave
like its historical predecessors. Here, for example, is
the faculty's response to a student strike called at one
university and spreading to others:

. . . the professors lament and snivel, imploring
the government not to take the road of reaction

and to make use of an excellent opportunity "to
ensure peace and order with the help of reforms"
in "a country exhausted by convulsions"—imploring the students not to resort to unlawful courses
which can only play into the hands of reaction,
etc., etc., etc. How ancient and antiquated, how
hackeneyed are all these tunes . . . .[14]

This is not a description of Columbia University in
1968. It is Lenin's description of St. Petersburg University in 1908. When Lenin describes even earlier
events, it sounds like the 1964 Free Speech Movement
at Berkeley and its aftermath: The liberal professors
join with the students to gain student freedom of
assembly and speech, but when the students invite
revolutionary off-campus speakers to their meetings
these same liberal professors run around denouncing
outside troublemakers; then they waver and dash from
one side to another, "urging the revolutionists to desist
from revolution, and the police to desist from reaction." [15]

More important than the similarity between the
behavior of American professors in the 1960s and Russian professors before 1910 is the similarity between
the behavior of each of these groups and the social
class to which they belong. Lenin raises the key questions: "Indeed, was the liberal professors' behaviour
before and during the Moscow events fortuitous? . . .
Does this behaviour express the individual peculiarities
of a given group of the liberal bourgeoisie, or does it
express the fundamental interests of this entire class

in general?" [16] Anyone familiar with the American liberal left in the 1960s must realize that the liberal faculty—and most faculties are now, as they were in Russia 60 years ago, overwhelmingly liberal—represents, and speaks for, a larger class within our society. This was well understood by Eugene McCarthy, who was the candidate of this class. (In France, this class has its own party, the Partie Socialiste Unifié, which successfully ran Mendes-France as a peace candidate to settle its war in Vietnam.) Some portions of the faculty are actually part of the ruling class, or consciously identify themselves with its interests. These are the faculty-administrators, the corporation lawyers who act as professors in the law school and the businessmen who act as professors in the business school, the research entrepeneurs, and many of the other hirelings of the "defense" department. But most of the faculty feels alienated from power, both within the university and in the society at large, and indeed they are. These are the middle-class professionals whose fate Marx and Engels accurately saw in 1848: "the physician, the lawyer, the priest, the poet, the man of science" become converted into "paid wage labourers." [17] As such, they are alienated from both the ruling class and the industrial working class, both of whom they fear and sometimes despise. This is the liberal faculty.

But there is a new ingredient in the faculty. Until fairly recently, only a few people without independent means of support could see their way through graduate school and join the professorial elite. But the demands of advanced capitalism for a highly educated labor force, the population explosion within the generation reaching college in the sixties, and the vastly expanded financial support from foundations, industry, state and federal government have all combined to change the internal class composition of the faculty. There has been wide recruiting of young people who before could not have been able to afford degrees, much less been able to penetrate the country club faculties. The wider class basis of the younger faculty creates new contradictions. Why, many of us do not even consider ourselves gentlemen. And some of us are beginning to identify clearly and openly not only with the American working class but with all the peoples of the world most oppressed and exploited by American imperialism. On the surface this looks like a generational gap. Last month at the annual convention of the Modern Language Association, which consists of college and university teachers of all the modern languages and literatures, a serious rebellion took place. It was a rebellion against the establishment, against tradition, against the prevailing ideas of what a professor should be, and against American imperialism. Louis Kampf of MIT was punched by a hotel detective and he and two others were arrested by the New York City police, who brought an entire busload of their forces to the main hotel. We not only had a sit-in to force the dropping of charges, but then elected Louis second vice president, which means that he plans the program for next year's convention and the following year will become president of the entire 28,000-member organization. We passed a number of resolutions, including one denouncing the U.S. war against the Vietnamese people as "illegal, immoral, and imperialistic," and demanding the immediate withdrawal of American and puppet forces. All the votes, both on Louis' election and on the rebels' resolutions, were standing votes; all therefore seemed glaring evidence of a generational conflict, with old and young now standing, now sitting. But all those who think that this conflict is primarily between age groups and that we will outgrow our present ideologies overlook two things—the past and the future. For such a rebellion is without precedent, and the forces behind it are growing each year. I do not support "faculty power" because it is abstractly legitimate, but only because and only insofar as it represents the power of the exploited and oppressed.

Trying to determine the class relations of college students is extremely difficult and complicated. First we must recognize the substantial differences among students at different kinds of schools. Carl Davidson makes the following distinctions:

> The traditional Ivy League schools shape the sons and daughters of the ruling class and old middle class into the new ruling and managerial elites. The state colleges and universities develop the sons and daughters of the working class and

petty bourgeoisie into the highly skilled sectors of the new working class, the middle sector white collar workers, and the traditional middle class professionals. Finally, the new community and junior colleges serve the increasing educational needs of, for the most part, the sons and daughters of the working class.[18]

This is generally accurate, but there are even more distinctions. Certainly in California there is a noticeable difference between the class backgrounds of those within the university system and those within the state college system, and the state tacitly and practically recognizes this difference, allocating for each student within the university several times the amount of money allocated for each student in the state colleges. Then there are small colleges and even junior colleges that cater exclusively to the children of the rich; there are the Negro colleges of the south and urban north; and there are programs to bring a token number of the poor, particularly poor blacks, into the most prestigious schools.

Sometimes overriding all these class distinctions is that role of student as nigger, combined with the rosy future lying before each student who can win out over his fellows. In a sense students are temporarily declassé, living in a limbo between their wealthy or working-class past and whatever careers they are being channeled into. Although physically and psychologically capable of working and childbearing, indeed more energetic and sexually motivated than many "adults," though often among the most intellectually alert and best informed members of society, they are branded by that society as immature parasites. They are generally not permitted either to sell their labor or to own property. Although they may work extremely hard in school, they are told this is not real work, that they are not working for a living, and that therefore they have essentially no rights. The used car salesman thinks of the premedical student as a chiseler living off his hard-earned money. Neither workers nor owners, students share some of the experience of the most clearly class-less elements of society, the true lumpenproletariat. Presumably this experience has some effect on their consciousness. At least they know what it is to be considered a parasite. Their class loyalties weaken. The sanctity of both work and private property is questioned. Of course they are still in part products of their natal class. But because their class position is now ambiguous, many of them pass as naturally into the lumpenproletariat as back into the class roles for which they supposedly were being trained. The sons and daughters of some of the wealthiest capitalists drop out; some take to the street in rebellious demonstrations, some as a way of life. Many identify with the life style and consciousness of the most oppressed, and take as their heroes Malcolm X, Huey Newton, Ho Chi Minh, Che Guevara, and Mao Tse-tung. And for many this is not some youthful aberration or fad, to be outgrown as soon as they realize that these values are not as attractive as suburbia.

To some extent, this has been true of students for a long time, and accounts for the essential role they have played in all twentieth century revolutionary struggle. Students acted as a catalytic agent of consciousness in the Russian, Chinese, and Cuban revolutions, as well as in the various wars of national liberation (even the Yugoslav partisans had strong student leadership). But advanced monopoly capitalism, by making huge quantitative changes, increases the role of students qualitatively. Its demands for highly skilled manpower, and virtually only highly skilled manpower, force it to educate unprecedented numbers of students to unheard-of levels of proficiency in understanding and manipulating abstract knowledge. And the demands of managing and rationalizing a worldwide empire create even greater needs. In all previous societies, university students were a chosen elect, the sons of the ruling class plus the most able sons of the professional and middle classes. Now university students are the sons and *daughters* of all classes except the lowest, which in the United States means racial minorities. And at this moment, of course, even the sons and daughters of blacks, Chicanos, and Indians are beginning to move into the universities. When we are talking about "students" we are now talking about a significant portion of the entire population. The number of college students now approximately equals the country's total armed forces plus its three largest unions (Teamsters, UAW, and United Steelworkers).

The widening class background of the younger faculty is amplified several times over among the students. So the most significant development now taking place among the student left is the rapid rise of a working-class orientation. This manifests itself in several ways. There are big debates as to whether professors are members of the working class, whether students themselves are, whether the concept of the "new working class" defines the roles of either. Graduate student labor organizing, particularly into militant AFT chapters, is growing rapidly. Students are exploring labor history and beginning to participate directly in strikes and organizing, particularly of the nonteaching employees on campus. A small but swiftly increasing number of students is going into industrial work in a conscious attempt to forge the missing link in a worker-student alliance. The slogan "student power" is being progressively rejected, except insofar as it represents an early form of the power of those without property and privilege.

On the campus there exists another group, rarely if ever thought of as a possible co-ruler of the university—the nonteaching employees. The lower strata of this group—janitors, gardeners, maintenance men, kitchen workers, maids, clerks, typists—include a far higher proportion of racial minorities, live in neighborhoods removed from the faculty and administration but often shared with students, particularly graduate students, and are the most direct representatives of the super-exploited. Generally these people are looked upon by all other groups within the university— administration, faculty, and students—as not being a part of the university. In fact, they come close to being invisible. As they organize, one demand that they will raise is that the educational facilities of the university be made available not only to their children but to them. If they were to win this demand, the effects would be extremely radical. Their presence in an economics class or a history class would *force* a change in the content of the course. Or take my own field. Most students at any one time are in classes on the novel, for good reason. The novel is the main art form of the bourgeoisie, rising with that class and mainly concerned with individual class status (from Richardson, Defoe, Fielding, and Jane Austen through Henry James to Faulkner, Malamud, Bellow, and Styron). Imagine the effects if that social class which to the bourgeois imagination seem merely objects to be escaped could actually participate in the discussion of these novels. And now suppose that the class to which these people belong had control over the resources of the university and thus determined the class content of its courses.

In the final analysis, there can be only one radical position: the overwhelming majority of people, that is, the working class, must run the universities. Very few students have reached the realization that only by struggling for workers' control of the university can they form a valid worker-student alliance. But they are getting there, as San Francisco State dramatically shows. And they will be increasingly influenced by the fact that all this has already happened for one quarter of the world's population. In the Cultural Revolution in China, students began by struggling for increased admission of workers and peasants to higher education, different class content in the courses, radical changes in testing and grading, and student power as opposed to faculty and administration power. As that struggle advanced, they closed down the schools and went to the workers and peasants to learn from them. What they learned was that only the workers and peasants had the power to make the changes they sought. The result is that the universities are now run by the workers and peasants and are totally at the service of the needs of the people, there is no longer a distinction between students and workers because everybody both works and studies, and the old Mandarin system of competitive testing has been eliminated and replaced by collective learning and collective evaluation.

The American course of development to the people's university will of course be quite different from the Chinese. This is how it will probably happen: The interpenetration of the university and the state will increase, rather than decrease. The present supposedly radical, but objectively reactionary, demand for university autonomy will be dropped by students and retained, if at all, only by liberal arts professors. The present supposedly conservative, but objectively progressive, demand for more control over the university by the political apparatus of the state now being made by the ruling-class politicians and press will soon become a middle-class demand, and it will then be implemented. The revolutionaries will gradually realize that this university-state synthesis contains the potential to meet all human material needs, and they will fight for a new form of this giant, to be under the control of the working people and poor people. Meanwhile the class composition of student bodies and faculties will continue to shift. This will be most noticeable in the form of an influx of racial minorities, who will increasingly identify themselves, as they have just started to do, as Third World people. The ruling class will escalate its present attempts to get white working class support against the students. Present examples of this in California are Reagan's overt appeals to the workers, and the administration of the College of San Mateo, which is forced to use an offer of increased admission of poor whites as a weapon against the Third World Liberation Front. But this ruling-class tactic will be self-defeating, for any substantial increase in working-class participation in the universities will weaken ruling-class dominance in the society as a whole. And the Third World people will increasingly recognize the fact that they are the vanguard of the entire working class, and they will build a growing alliance with white workers. If all this sounds far-fetched, go to San Francisco State and watch the white truck drivers pull up to the picket line, raise a clenched fist, and turn their trucks around.

REBUTTALS

H. BRUCE FRANKLIN

When I read Dr. Howard's paper, I received two surprises. First, it was not a totally liberal analysis. Second, because of this, he and I had some rather important areas of agreement. Perhaps one could say that although he was attacking liberalism from the right while I was attacking it from the left, we share some of the same dissatisfaction with liberal premises and goals.

Dr. Howard cited a three-year survey of 7,500 professors and administrators which had demonstrated that their number one objective was to "Protect the faculty's right to academic freedom." When I read this, I assumed that he was going to agree, and so I scribbled down an exposé of the fallacy behind that objective. Then I turned the page and found that he had already exposed one sham behind "the present orthodoxy" that the university's transcendent mission is the pure and disinterested " 'pursuit of truth.' " In his words:

> Knowledge, of itself, has no value. It is only the use to which man puts his knowledge that gives it value. By treating the pursuit of knowledge as the noblest endeavor and a self-justifying endea-

vor and one which must never be confined, we have lost track of the meaning and the consequences of the educational process.

Dr. Howard then argues that the university should teach values, that it should have as one of its main goals what he calls "character education." I would agree with this and go even further to assert that a university cannot help but teach values and provide some kind of character education. As he himself points out elsewhere, the faculty, because of its very pretense to ethical neutrality, effectively teaches one set of ethics: "If the highest priority of our educational system is to have every faculty member do his own thing without limits and without regard to the views or the interests of anyone else, we really shouldn't be surprised if the students, and particularly the brightest ones, get the message and decide to do their own thing without limits and without regard to anyone else." Unlike Dr. Howard, I would call this the very quintessence of the bourgeois ethic and the bourgeois conweek, the multiversity is permeated by the bourgeois workers without restraint, the freedom to privately own public property, the freedom to buy medical care, justice, and political office in the marketplace, the freedom to pollute the air and water, the freedom to use the world's resources to make and sell useless or deadly trash, the freedom to conscript an army to fight for an economic empire, or, on the other side, it is the freedom to sell your life's labor to the highest bidder and even to scab, the freedom to compete for grades and rank, and the freedom to protest against the draft while you are being dragged away. As I pointed out last week, the multiversity is permeated by the bourgeois ethic of competition, with each person in it pitted against his fellows. Or in Dr. Howard's words: "To a significant degree, each man is in opposition to all the rest."

I find my own experience instructive here. Before I became a Communist, I had the values I was supposed to have in regard to my own professional publication. That is, I was eager to rush into print to be first with a discovery, to be "original"; I was anxious lest someone else should beat me to it. Now I always hope that many other people will reach the same conclusions that I have and get them into print so that I can perform other duties. It was interesting last week that some people thought they were annihilating my position by pointing out that they had heard similar ideas in the 1930s. I am not embarrassed but joyful to share the ideas of the greatest people of that era, ideas that are now shared by the overwhelming majority of the world's population that has considered these problems.

Dr. Howard concluded his paper with a quotation that affirmed what he called "the true purpose" of the university, which " 'exists to make a fellowship by means of which standards of civilization will be erected and the progress of civilization will be enhanced.' " Nobody could possibly argue with this, though we certainly might have some hot debates about its meaning and application. As Dr. Howard said in the discussion, "Everybody is for excellence, like motherhood." It seems to me that he interprets this in a formalist way. That is, he conceives of a fixed structure and then defines the internal relationships of that structure. (It is strikingly similar to the way New Criticism makes the students read a poem.) On top are the trustees; beneath them is the president, who is really the philosopher-king; then comes the faculty; on the bottom are the students. I think the important questions are not dealt with, for implicit in his concept of this structure is a commitment to the status quo. Would he be equally happy if his formula for university power were followed in China or the Soviet Union? Should their universities be run by powerful presidents carrying out the objectives prescribed by a governing board? You see, the important questions are: Who are the people in these various roles? and How do they relate to other groups in our own society and in the world?

Our question is not whether the university should teach values and build character. We agree on this, but disagree profoundly on *whose* values, what kind of character. I am arguing that the university should be building Socialist and Communist character, that is, that it should be teaching what is of value to poor and working people, not because this is abstractly "better" but because this comes from and meets the needs of the people. It should be teaching solidarity, communality, and brotherhood rather than competition and alienation; it should be helping to develop popular culture instead of forcing people to grovel before elitist culture or wallow in a culture of despair; it should be enriching the vulgar and eloquent language of the people rather than emasculating our expression with bourgeois rules of grammar and decadent formalism; it should be a means of liberating the classes on the bottom rather than enriching the one true minority group in our society, the little group on top.

Whereas Dr. Howard sees our university and college system as thoroughly pluralistic, I think that it teaches the culture and ideology of only the bourgeoisie and previous ruling classes. At this point, Dr. Howard falls into the very liberalism he had earlier attacked, suggesting that each college and university do its own thing (although implicitly setting rather narrow limits on what kind of thing). As I indicated last week, the universities cannot do their own thing, because they use and produce vast resources of the society, they are essential sources and instruments of power, and they are irreversibly interpenetrating with the other main political and economic institutions of the society. The values they teach, that is, the values of the exploiting class, are now confronting other values, irreconcilably conflicting values, the values of the exploited classes. The ideology of almost every department of every American university and college is being met head-on by the ideology of the masses of the Third

World, and every one of us will have to choose sides in this struggle.

Dr. Howard sees one main cause behind "the financial peril" of the university as well as its "other deep and grievous difficulties . . . the disruptions and takeovers and in-fighting"; all this he sees as "the result of a failure of presidential leadership to hold high before the academic community the purposes of its existence and insist upon action appropriate to these purposes." I would be considerably more charitable to university presidents, for I think that Dr. Howard has reversed cause and effect. What he is describing is the breakdown of an ideology, and I would agree. But institutions do not break down because their leading spokesmen and administrators get ideologically confused. The process works the opposite way. An ideology breaks down when the system it is supposed to rationalize develops objective contradictions too extreme to handle. This explains why last week the ideologues for the system were unable to confront my argument directly, and why they lapsed into peripheral quibbles and irrational ad hominem arguments, even going as far as to call me a Trotskyist and a revisionist. They could not come right out and say that the universities *should* be run by the rich and that the people should *not* run the universities. That ideology, once virtually unquestioned, has been made virtually unmentionable by the changing class relationships I described last week. Instead, they had to villify the working class without letting it appear that they did not believe in democracy, the rule of the people. The working class supports the Vietnam war, votes for Wallace, and uses bad grammar; therefore it is not necessary to take seriously the argument that they should run the universities. Now these gentlemen know as well as I do that it was not the working class that started the Vietnam war and led the people into tolerating it, that only a tiny minority of them voted for Wallace,[1] and that neither Shakespeare nor Melville wrote grammatically. My point here is not to insult the intelligence of those arguing with me; quite the reverse, I would like them to understand that it was the internal contradictions in their ideology that forced them into irrationality.

I believe a similar phenomenon can be seen in Dr. Howard's position, for it, like that of other presidents, is founded upon contradictions, contradictions coming directly from the objective world. The internal contradictions of bourgeois ideology can never be apparent to those who most passionately affirm it, because it rests on that primal exercise of brute power and violence, the expropriation for private use of the labor and resources of the entire population.

Each of the five rules Dr. Howard lays down for the governance of the university papers over deep contradictions:

1. The first rule distinguishes between two kinds of free speech, that accorded to those acceptable to the power structure and a much less significant kind

granted to others. "The university"—and this apparently means the president—"sees fit to invite" certain people to speak on campus. These chosen few are given a podium, publicity, an auditorium, and an audience. The rest of the people on the campus are supposed to give them a respectful hearing, may ask questions unless these are "attempts to harass or embarrass" the speaker, but may not protest, even on a silent picket sign. There seems to be no provision at all for those who wish to speak and are not authorized to do so by the "university."

2. The second rule calls for "the rejection of emotionalism and sensationalism" because they "are antithetical to the conduct of intellectual endeavor." The segregation of emotion and intellect is, of course, necessary to a system based on exploitation and inequality; we are supposed to understand such facts dispassionately, not respond to them with the appropriate emotions. This alienation is the essential act of dehumanization that prevents us from comprehending such an intellectual fact as the body count of Vietnamese peasants. That is why our political science departments and economics departments work so hard to construct abstract, ethically neutral models.

3. "The prohibition of the physical capture of university premises or university employees by college personnel." But the fact is that all the university premises and almost all the university employees have already been physically captured, and this is the central con-

tradiction of the university, its embodiment of that primal bourgeois expropriation. Stanford University, for instance, comes directly from Leland Stanford's money which came directly from land stolen from the Indians and Mexicans and labor stolen from Chinese immigrants. It is fueled, as I showed last week, by the wealth of the Pacific Basin, which it is consciously and explicitly trying to turn into an economic empire. In the past few years at Stanford, one building housed an experimental college developed by the students and another, the Old Union, was the undergraduate dormitory universally acknowledged to be the most intellectually exciting student residence on campus. The administration, using its virtually unchallenged power, physically captured the experimental college building, thus destroying the experimental college, and turned it into the Placement Office, where interviews are held for employment with the CIA, Dow Chemical, and the many other parts of the war machine represented on the board of trustees. If the students who were evicted from that building were to sit in to protest, Dr. Howard, like the administration and most of the faculty at Stanford, would call this act, unlike the other, a "physical capture of university premises." When the administration decided to seize the Old Union and turn it into an office building for itself, there was a protest. My own department, for instance, submitted a petition signed by almost every faculty member pointing out that the administration was about to destroy a unique intellectual center, the most productive meeting place on campus for faculty and students. The administration did not even deign to issue a formal reply. Then last year this building was the scene of the big sit-in protesting the high-handed suspension of seven students involved in a peaceful demonstration against CIA recruiting on campus. The participants in the sit-in very pointedly obstructed no one's entrance to the building, guaranteed the safety and functioning of all offices, and carefully kept the floors and washrooms clean. Yet this, unlike the earlier expropriation, was seen not only as a physical capture but as an act of violence and anarchy. The arguments were precisely those used by management in Flint, Michigan, in 1936, where the sit-in tactic was pioneered by the auto workers. Though it was the labor of the workers that had built the factories, the owners and managers, together with their press and their politicians, could see their own occupation of the factories as the only imaginable condition of an orderly and lawful society.[2] A factory or a university occupied and run by anybody but the bourgeoisie seems to them the epitome of anarchy.

Dr. Howard's other two rules concern "the university's general obligations in the present context of society":

1. ". . . in every aspect of the university, there shall be no discrimination on the basis of race, color or religion." Let us note the unspoken exceptions to this

rule. Entrance requirements are to be such that very few members of racial minorities and the working class in general can qualify. Verbal aptitude tests, for instance, are to be designed to see how well the student can read and write the language of the bourgeoisie. The knowledge to be taught is that which the bourgeoisie considers important: it is important to know Beethoven, Wordsworth, and T. S. Eliot, but not Leadbelly, Woodie Guthrie, and Bob Dylan; Plato, Darwin, and Paul Samuelson, but not Mao Tse-Tung; the operation of a laboratory distillation apparatus, but not that of an automobile engine; the art of cathedral windows, but not that of political posters; the history of Europe, but not that of Africa. (This may sound to your ears anti-intellectual, whereas in fact it is merely anti-elitist.) Dr. Howard seems unconscious of what he is confessing when he boasts that once his college brought "70 of the world's foremost Negroes to our campus" for four or five days because "it was high time that somebody dramatized and rejoiced in the incredible contributions which Negroes had made to our society." One reason black people are demanding autonomous black studies departments is that people like Dr. Howard, no matter how earnest their motives, cannot comprehend their own unconscious racial discrimination. If this sounds harsh, examine his own institution. In looking at Rockford's curriculum, I used a 1963/64 catalog, the latest available at Stanford; I'm sure that some improvements have since been made, largely because of what Dr. Howard calls those left-wing "Quixotic assaults upon the institutions of society." Dr. Howard says that "there shall be no discrimination on the basis of race [or] color" "in every aspect of the university." The curriculum of Rockford says in effect, "We don't discriminate on the basis of race or culture; it's just that other cultures aren't quite as good as ours and only our history is important." Every single history course deals with the history of Europe and the United States. The music department teaches the theory and history of white music only. In all the literature departments, there is only one course in non-white literature, a course in Asian literature "given when elections justify"; I understand from Dr. Howard's earlier remarks that there is now an interim course in literature of the black revolution. The art department offers at least five courses in the history of "Western" art, allowing only one stain to show through the whitewash, a course entitled "Primitive Art" and thus described in the catalog: "Survey of the arts of the African Negro, the Oceanic peoples and the North American Indians." What kind of thought but racist thought could classify the art of, say, the Ashanti civilization as "primitive"? This cultural racism perfectly illustrates what I referred to last week as the kind of knowledge useful only to the class that produced it; by making supposedly objective classifications it rationalizes white supremacy and teaches black people that they are some kind of naked savage in disguise.

2. Dr. Howard's only other rule on "the university's general obligations in the present context of society" is: "A commitment on the part of the university to observe public law and to cooperate with public authorities in maintaining public law." Now the question, whether the university should support what is legal or what is just when the two conflict, is precisely the heart of the issue in much of the present moral protest and confrontation. But Dr. Howard is forced by the contradiction in his argument to deal with this parenthetically as follows: "(The whole question of the university's tolerance or encouragement of civil disobedience needs a thorough airing, but that is another speech.)"

The fact is that the neutrality of the university is a sham, just as the neutrality of bourgeois law and order is a sham. The university, as we all know, or at least as the Department of Defense knows, is an integral part of the war machine. Dr. Howard gives this away when he names the first qualification of today's ideal university president:[3] "The enormous variety of federal programs for higher education, and the enormous volume of federal funds that flows to the campus, and the dependence of the university upon these funds make it desirable that the head of any major university have, as one of his principal qualifications, a wealth of contacts in Washington and a reputation which will earn him appointments to the Board of the National Science Foundation, Presidential Task Forces or other posts of distinction and visibility within the government." Dr. Howard sees a fundamental identity between the government and the people. When he says that the university must work "in harmony with the interests of the public or the government," he means that they are the same thing. But the majority of the world's population makes a clear distinction between the American people and the American government, which they look upon as their number one enemy.

The hidden contradiction becomes apparent when Dr. Howard deals with the substance of student dissent:

> Students are demanding that the university abandon its neutrality, take sides and take action concerning the great moral issues of our times. Students have demanded that the universities withdraw from the Institute for Defense Analysis and prohibit recruiters from the military services and recruiters from the manufacturers of napalm and refuse to do business with commercial enterprises which support South Africa.

Since Dr. Howard has just attacked the present university philosophy, according to which "the university may just as readily graduate an Adolph Hitler as an Albert Schweitzer" and since he says that these student demands are aimed precisely at this "neutrality," the logical conclusion to this argument would be to say either that these students are right or that the university *should* aid in the manufacture of napalm, military recruiting, and apartheid. But he cannot do this.

Like those he criticizes, he takes an apparently neutral
position, which is effectively a position of support, on
the university's involvement with napalm, the Vietnam
war, and apartheid. Then he characterizes the activist
students as merely "leading Quixotic assaults upon the
institutions of society" and claims, quite contrary to
fact, that on "the other end of the youth spectrum"
are "the young people who are blazing trails in harmony with and as a part of society—the Peace Corpsmen, the tutors of underprivileged students, and other
dedicated social servants." Everybody with any contact with large numbers of the radical activists knows
that these are the very same people who did civil rights
work in the rural south and the urban north, first
stirred the conscience of the nation about Vietnam,
and served in the Peace Corps and Vista. On the opposite end of the youth spectrum from these selfless
heroes are the ambitious, the avaricious, the blood-
thirsty, and the gung-ho.

Dr. Howard thinks that by banning "student organizations committed to the use of violence," the president can restore order. The only student organizations
I know that are committed to violence are ROTC and
the football team, neither of which I believe is to be
found at Rockford. I suspect that he is really alluding
to SDS, which is no more committed to violence than
any non-pacifist political organization, including the
Republican and Democratic parties. In order to restore order, it would be necessary to ban the causes

of disorder, which are also the causes of revolutionary organizations, a label that before long will probably describe SDS accurately. As a revolutionary myself, I really don't care much one way or the other if SDS is banned. That would make practical organizing activity a little more inconvenient, but it would expedite revolutionary cadre formation. I would, however, welcome a successful ban on the main cause of disorder, because that would mean that the revolution has triumphed. For the greatest cause of disorder in the history of man is capitalism. This disorder is by no means entirely a bad thing, however, as I tried to indicate in my paper last week. In the words of the *Communist Manifesto:*

> Constant revolutionizing of production, uninterrupted disturbance of all social conditions, everlasting uncertainty and agitation distinguish the bourgeois epoch from all earlier ones. All fixed, fast frozen relations, with their train of ancient and removable prejudices and opinions, are swept away, all new-formed ones become antiquated before they can ossify. All that is solid melts into air, all that is holy is profaned, and man is at last compelled to face with sober senses his real conditions of life and his relations with his kind.

JOHN A. HOWARD

Arthur Godfrey told a story recently which bears on my position at the moment. A barfly suddenly announced in a loud, thick voice that he held in his hand a list of all those present whom he could lick with one hand tied behind him. A very large, impressive beer-drinker stalked over to the braggert and asked if his name was on the list. The barfly checked his list and said, "Yes, here's your name right here!" The other fellow replied that if the little fellow thought he could beat him up, he was mistaken. "Is that so?" said the little one forcefully. "Then I guess I had better remove your name from my list."

In the present confrontation, I am not sure whether I should take Dr. Franklin's name off my list. I supposed I could hold my own in a discussion of the relationships between the various constituencies of the university. In his approach to the topic, he has chosen to argue ideologies and provide recommendations for university organization by referring us to a system of education about which little is generally known. I am not a Marxist scholar and I certainly am not equipped to discuss the plusses and minuses of the Chinese people's universities, but I will offer some observations about those matters where there are points of contact between his paper and mine and the topic assigned.

It is evident that Professor Franklin and I share certain basic views on this topic. We agree that the determination of who should run the university should be made according to a fundamental judgment about the nature of the society which the university is to serve. Both of us perceive that the changes now taking place in the university are influences counter to the kind of society to which I am committed and toward the kind of society to which he is committed. (And I welcome his assistance in drawing this matter to the attention of the public.) Both of us recognize that the increasing role of the federal government in higher education has contributed to the decline of private enterprise capitalism and individual initiative. We both recognize that the modern university is relatively disinterested in its enrolled students. He concludes, as I do, that the university should be at the service of the needs of the people.

I do, however, detect certain points on which there may be some disagreement.

In the first place, I believe man is most creative when to produce in a manner that will benefit himself and to produce in a manner that will benefit himself and his family. It is said that many a young instructor has been spurred on to towering heights of brilliance and

early promotion in the hope of being relieved of eight
o'clock classes. The opportunity to better one's situation is a powerful stimulus. I also believe man is so
constituted that he has the potential for deriving pleas-
ure from being of service to someone else. As living
conditions are conducive to the fulfillment of these
two human impulses man is able to build a productive
society and to earn personal satisfaction and self-esteem.

The political and economic systems which developed
in this country were uniquely supportive of these two
human characteristics, serving well and capitalizing
upon the pluralistic nature of our population, providing more favorable circumstances than any other society ever has for a person to improve his position
according to his own talents and persistence, also giving
rise to an incredibly diverse complex of private service
agencies, and nourishing the altruistic impulse in the
people. Anyone who supposes the popular support of
the Marshall Plan was simply a reflection of self-inter-
est doesn't understand America.

It happened that the educational system which
evolved in our country was also magnificently able to
support and capitalize upon the diversity of our population. Each local school district and each college and
university was responsible to its own board of control
and that board was free to make decisions according to
its evaluation of local needs and local circumstances and
according to the values and the aspirations of that community. To be sure, the system had certain terrible

and cruel failings, but on the national level it has provided the most comprehensive, the most creative and
the most flexible total program of education of any
nation for which factual information is available.

The success of the system was, in my judgment, in
large part the consequence of the autonomy of the
schools and the opportunity for each to find its own
answers to problems, and the result of the potential for
any school to rise by its own efforts to heights of prestige and accomplishment. Does anyone suppose, for
instance, that if education were, in the first half of this
century, centrally planned and centrally paid for that
a Carleton College or a Reed College or a Swarthmore
College would have emerged from the great number
of little known colleges to a position of international
eminence, or that the innovations and creative work
which earned them such stature would have taken place?
I think not. And that is why I presented in my earlier
paper an analysis based upon the determination and
implementation of individual policy according to the
judgments of each institution for itself.

I reject, as less creative and less useful to mankind,
any system of centrally determined education, whether
the determination is made by an enlightened office of
education, the military-industrial establishment, or a
somehow codified will of the working class.

Next, I would like to suggest that Mr. Franklin and
his fellow radicals may underestimate the instincts for

self-preservation and the ability of the American people to respond to attack.

Americans are extraordinarily tolerant and patient and slow to react, but there comes a point beyond which they will not sit idly by. I attended a conference last summer in which a number of student officers were discussing student activism. At one point a member of the audience challenged the student from Columbia University and urged him to use the proper designations in referring to what he and the other protesters had done. He said the students had committed a number of crimes, such as breaking and entering, looting, etc. The student replied that in a revolution there are no crimes and that this was revolution. From there on, the audience paid close attention and listened carefully. And I am certain that those present will henceforth take a wholly different view of student activism.

It is naive to suppose that the American public is going to support indefinitely institutions and activities which are patently directed to the destruction of the society which is paying the bills. There is a growing unwillingness on the part of taxpayers, state and national legislation, alumni, and the general populace to permit the universities to be divided and disrupted by coercive minorities. It is to be hoped that rational and deliberative techniques can be used to restore order so that the universities can spend their time on the proper business of universities instead of self-defense. However, if rational techniques are not effective, other techniques will be employed, albeit reluctantly. The use of force breeds counter-force. The free nations tried too long to arrive at some rational accord with Hitler, but eventually they turned to force to put a stop to his depredation. Hitler underestimated the nerve and the vitality of free institutions. I believe the radicals who are overtly trying to overthrow our universities make the same miscalculation. The apathy runs deep, but not that deep.

Another observation I would like to make has to do with our differing views of the classes of society. Professor Franklin seems to imply that the laboring man and the have-nots have a monopoly on virtue and those who own some property or occupy positions of influence have a monopoly on vice. This is patently ridiculous. We agree that acquiring property brings a certain kind of power, but we disagree on the consequences of the acquisition. People do desire things and once having them, they wish to protect them. We have built a society which takes these human attitudes into account and which aspires to make it possible for each person to get a share of the action with the resulting gratifications for himself. To the degree that we can deliver on our aspiration for an open society, Professor Franklin's concept will be thwarted.

Further, I am intrigued by what seems to be an implication of his statement. I make the supposition that education will add to the individual's capacity to achieve power, with or without property. If the achievement of power is, in his view, undesirable, is it then the purpose of education to divest the student of his talents and his natural advantage so that he cannot achieve power and will live in virtuous poverty and powerlessness? It may be possible by government action to eliminate private property, or keep redistributing it, but I do not believe it is possible to even out human talents and brains and initiative and persistence. Some people are naturally going to achieve more than others. If achievement is to be feared and suppressed, it poses a rather dismal view of man and his future.

A related point has to do with the selection of trustees and regents. If there is something inherently sinister in the selection of highly successful people to make the ultimate decisions for the university, here again we encounter a paradox. It seems to me that the institution which is established to deal with man's brain and man's performance ought to be guided by people who, by their own record, are strong on brains and strong on performance. I also challenge his assertion that "the trustees and regents so far have been able to make sure that only the culture and ideology of their own class and of previous ruling classes can be propagated in their universities." My authority for this challenge is Professor Franklin's own statement. He says "most faculties are now, as they were in Russia 60 years ago, overwhelmingly liberal." If anyone supposes that trustees and regents across the country are overwhelmingly liberal, he ought to travel a little and meet some.

The discrepancy between the basic economic and political attitudes of the trustees and of the faculty is not, I believe, the manifestation of a failure on the part of trustees to impose their views and to govern universities in a fashion that will make little carbon copies of themselves, but rather a sign of the virtue of trustees generally in recognizing that society changes and education must change with it and that academic freedom is the stuff of creative education. I think the record of university trustees in this country proves the opposite of Dr. Franklin's assertion. And, as will be noted from my earlier comments, that may not be a wholly unmixed blessing.

Our universities, as now constituted, may be slow to change, but they are geared to consider and present new ideas and to assist and participate in changes in society and changes in their own operation. The recent restructuring of the policy boards of a number of major Catholic universities, replacing priests with laymen, is dramatic evidence that our universities are not frozen into the original concept and pattern.

On the other hand, I note Dr. Franklin's allusion to Jerry Farber's satire, "Students are Niggers," which bemoans our system of education wherein many decisions are made for the students and students must docilely accept those decisions. I know all too little about the people's universities of Communist China which are held up to us as models, but I cannot help wondering whether the students over there are required to accept without challenge the teachings of Chairman Mao. I have the impression that the chairman's conclusions about man and society are regarded as the ultimate word and are not open to challenge. If such is the case, our system, with all its imperfections, may be better suited to adaptation and change, which both of us champion, than is the Chinese system.

Next, I am intrigued by Professor Franklin's enthusiasm for having the working people determine university decisions and academic content. I am not clear on where he draws the line on who deserves to be called "virtuous working people," and who has passed over the terrible line into oppressive management, but whether foremen are in the one class or the other, I am a little apprehensive about having even the foremen determine which novels are to be studied in a literature class or which text is to be used to teach atomic physics. I should think that even the Communist Chinese would recognize that certain people have the knowledge and the experience to make better decisions in their field of competence than untrained and inexperienced people, however virtuous or oppressed they may be.

This leads me to observe that the question to which we were originally asked to respond continues to require an answer. Whatever view one takes of social structures and man's destiny, the university in each society is still composed of students, teachers, managers, and policymakers. The interaction and the chain of command and the quality of the relationship among these components will inevitably control the volume and the quality of educational output, whatever the proclaimed purpose of the university may be. I have tried to suggest a manner in which these constituencies may most effectively operate together to serve well in our society. Professor Franklin has responded to the question in a different manner. He has, it seems to me, expressed his view that our society is not a good society and that our universities simply reflect and reenforce the undesirable society that we have. Hence he perceives it to be a waste of time to try to reorder the parts of the university, for that would be merely to reshuffle ill-conceived components. Even so, I insist that the initial question will still need answering in the ideal people's university. The relationships must still be sorted out and fitted into some kind of a hierarchy.

To conclude, it seems to me that the decentralized system of education which we have had in this country in the past has many basic virtues which are worth rescuing from the present thrust toward centralism. There is no question but what it is incumbent upon educational institutions to correct the deficiencies of the past, particularly with regard to equalizing opportunities for all students, but I am confident that it will not be necessary to destroy the system to make those corrections.

To lead the individual universities from the difficulties in which they now find themselves, I suggest again that it must be the president who runs the university, and that he must be a comprehensivist who can effectively serve as theorist, interpreter, implementer, and judge of the purposes of the institution. Simply to keep everything flowing smoothly in a university is a difficult task, but that is not sufficient to produce good education.

In any society, the university must have as a major function, the production of graduates competent to live productively in that society. In a free society, the pressures and the options and the challenges to the individual are infinitely greater than they are in a closed society so that when education fails, the failure of the student is the greater. Thus this discussion and all others directed to improving the effectiveness of the university are of the greatest import not just for educators, but for all thoughtful citizens.

I am grateful to the American Enterprise Institute for sponsoring this series and for inviting me to participate, and I am grateful to Professor Franklin for posing such an extraordinary challenge to which to respond.

DISCUSSION

FIRST SESSION

HAROLD ORLANS, Brookings Institution: I have two brief questions. I wonder if you would care to say anything at all beyond the few words that you said about the conceivable function of the faculty, since I suspect that our next speaker may make a little bit more of the faculty than you have. You have spoken far more about the functions of students than you have about the faculty.

Secondly, do you see any alternatives for different institutions? You have given us one picture for a strong president. What if a president at some institutions absolutely insists that he wants to share his power with one or another group? What if the circumstances of some kinds of colleges might even indicate a different course? Would you refuse a mission to him?

DR. HOWARD: First let me remind you that the debate topic is "Who Should Run the Universities?" This is all presented as an ideal.

Let me take the second question first. I would be the last person to suggest that there has to be a prototype and that everybody should adapt himself to it.

It seems to me that the genius of the educational system which has evolved in this country has been the autonomy of each institution to respond to its own circumstances and to do its own creating. One of my gravest concerns about the direction in which education has been moving in recent years is that there has been less and less autonomy and more and more similarity. I certainly would envision all kinds of variations.

You may know of the experiment at Black Mountain College where the students made the major decisions as to who should be appointed to the faculty and who should be reappointed. The college failed.

Some of the free universities connected with campuses around the country are endeavoring to create student-run organizations where courses and faculty are determined by student decisions.

I think there must be variety in order to serve a pluralistic society. But I think that there is an appropriate generalization to be made. Ideally there will be one person who knows what is going on everywhere, throughout the institution, who makes it his business to know, and who is responsible for the most critical decisions. I don't think anything I said precluded great variations in the amount of responsibility which is delegated. I think this will be and must be.

No institution is going to exist without a faculty, even a free university. And no good faculty is going to exist without some significant control over its own destiny.

I think the thing that I was trying to drive at was that faculty decision making should occur within a planned framework rather than without any significant or understood framework.

Let me try to offer some specific illustrations about the college which I serve. We have had some significant changes in our academic program in the nine years I have been there. One thing we do is to close the whole college down for four or five days every two years to engage in an all-college festival or symposium where faculty, students, administration, everybody—devotes energies to a theme that we think is of great importance to all of us.

In 1964, a long time before Selma, for instance, our college decided that we wanted to do something important with regard to the question of race relations. Everybody was stewing around about the problems between the races, and we thought it was high time somebody dramatized and rejoiced in the incredible contributions which Negroes had made to our society. We brought 70 of the world's foremost Negroes to our campus for five days. And they didn't just come and do their thing and go. Some stayed the whole time. We brought Olatunji and Company, the Nigerian dance troupe that was at the New York World's Fair. We brought editors of two of the Johnson publications, I can't remember whether it was *Ebony* and *Jet* or *Jet* and *Tan*. We brought William Warfield, legislators, jazz singers, and so forth.

These projects are proposed by the faculty and students and determined by the faculty and students. When proposed, I get involved in the deliberations. I try to suggest certain limits that may be there in terms of my perception of our budget.

When I go back to the campus, we will be doing one of these programs on humor. The faculty and the students have chosen the theme and participants. We think that if ever there was a time when man needed really to understand and appreciate and use his sense of humor, it is now, when we are all so polarized on so many things.

We have undertaken a four-one-four calendar which provides January Interim Programs. The faculty and the students determine the preceding spring which topics we will be offering, for the students to study solidly for the month of January, on our campus or off.

Many of the major innovations are initiated by faculty and students. I am not reluctant to suggest some of my own. But all of this kind of thing is wholly within the purview, responsibility, and initiative of the faculty.

STEPHEN HORN, Brookings Institution: You mentioned the great emphasis placed in this recent study on academic freedom. Related to that, of course, is academic tenure to preserve freedom and to protect faculty members.

I wonder what your thoughts and prognostications are concerning the quest of students today for excellence in curricula versus the resistance that academic tenure causes in bringing changes about within a university structure. Do you foresee, or do you advocate perhaps, reducing the amount of academic tenure? What would your judgment be as to the consequences of that action?

My own suspicion is that one of these days students will catch on to the idea that this might be at the root of some of their problems.

DR. HOWARD: A number of spokesmen have predicted that really the ultimate conflict is between students and faculty. It has not been recognized yet, but that is where we are heading.

First of all, much of our problem is that everybody talks about excellence but nobody knows what it is. At many of the professional meetings in higher education, if one examines the agenda, over and over and over again we find ourselves talking about the mechanics of education, such things as better utilization of teaching machines, fuller utilization of the calendar and facilities, foreign travel, finances, academic freedom, and so forth. Now, all of these things are critically important in the educational process but they are still the mechanics. You can improve their efficiency, but if nobody knows the destination, the speed at which the educational vehicle is traveling is of no consequence. What I am trying to suggest is that if you have identified the mission of the institution, then you give meaning to the term excellence.

This is part of the terrible confusion we are involved in now. Everybody is for excellence, like motherhood. But we don't have any frame of reference to determine what we mean by it.

As far as tenure is concerned, I don't see much likelihood that it is going to be reduced. It was instituted to protect the academic person against whimsical or biased judgments. I think this is a sound basis. I also think that when you really get down to the nitty gritty, tenure protects the weak man, particularly now when we have a shortage of good people in the country. A strong person who has lots of talents isn't going to stay very long at a place where he isn't wanted by the people who control the budget and are running the place. He is going to have lots of opportunities to go elsewhere.

I don't think that fact denies the original validity of the concept of tenure. But it seems to me that the big battles will not be about such matters as tenure. Remember, I assume that each university, in choosing its own mission and spelling it out, would define its mission somewhat differently from the next. Actually every educational institution in the country is quite different from every other.

I think most of us make the assumption that one good liberal arts college is much like another, or one good large university is much like another. This isn't true. Let us represent higher education as a pie diagram. Let's cut it one way in terms of the major thrust of the curriculum, and I'll deal with the liberal arts colleges because I know them best. At one end of the bisecting line you have Scripps College in California and St. John's in the East where the central thrust is on humanities. Cal Tech and MIT are at the other end. Everyone else is spread out along this axis representing the major curricular emphasis.

Cut our pie another way: How important is religion? In some institutions still, all major policies are evaluated according to their impact on religious objectives. At others, religion is a matter of supreme indifference. And we are all spread out along the line.

Cut it another way: What is the racial mix? Cut it another way: What is the mix of the economic background of the students? Cut it another way: What about fraternities and sororities?

And you can go on cutting that pie indefinitely. You must examine the location on each of those axes to learn the real character of each institution.

Now, I think again that this great and fundamental diversity has very well served our pluralistic society.

I think the students must be and will be in on the rephrasing or the phrasing of the purposes of the institution if institutions go the direction which I have suggested.

Then, as students exert pressures, it may be toward the commonly identified goals. If they want to go against these goals, okay, then universities must face that fact head on, and work with the students to decide whether the original goal is right, or wrong, or whether it was right at a previous time and ought to be changed now.

I think that this is the kind of ebb and flow and the kind of confrontation that is probably ahead of us rather than battling over a mechanic like tenure or over a vague term like excellence.

FREEMAN HOLMER, Council of State Governments: As you describe the role of the president of a university you describe it in terms which I can recognize as having particular relevance to Rockford College and to other colleges and smaller universities.

As I think about the problems of a large state university, however, particularly those with multiple campuses, etc., the role of the president who presides over a series of campuses is somewhat different.

DR. HOWARD: There is no question about this.

MR. HOLMER: Would you comment on that?

DR. HOWARD: I am fully aware of the limitations of my own experience. I have worked primarily in small colleges. I have attended for a significant period of time three universities and taught briefly in one. But my administrative experience is confined to the small colleges.

I think it is interesting that for this debate we have a man who, so far as I know, has never had any experience in administering an educational institution and a man who is an administrator of a small college. That is why at the beginning I said I was going to talk about any institution that grants a baccalaureate degree.

I know my limitations. I assume the audience hearing this knows them too. I simply cannot answer intelligently the question you are raising except as I examine this statement by university administrators of what they perceive to be their goals. As you look down that list and discover that aside from maintaining the intellectual competence of the students, the concern about what the student is and what he does and what is happening to him is registered toward the bottom of the list. This suggests to me that the thing I am saying here has real merit for the large university too. It is no wonder the students are up in arms, if what is happening to them is thirty-first or forty-sixth on the list.

I think somebody else with different qualifications must respond to your question but I will say, yes, the problem is very different.

WALTER B. GARVER, Retired: I think you have done a better job pointing to some goals and some objectives than I have seen for a long time. I sometimes think the problem is who can run them rather than who should, "should" involving a value judgment. You have raised doubts as to the qualifications of boards and regents.

My question is: Who, after all, is the real keeper of the flame? Who keeps the vision and who is going to get this thing back out of the woods if we are truly lost? If you have to depend on doubtful regents and trust .es, if presidents have become more money-raisers and negotiators than administrators, if they have become specialists just following their own noses, who is watching the road and knows where we are going?

DR. HOWARD: May I answer this in two ways. I think that the whole pace of our society has been accelerated and that many people in positions of leadership in government, in industry and education and everywhere else have been subjected to more and more demands. Increasingly the leaders in all elements of our society have understandably devoted their attention to implementing, to adjudicating, just to keeping the thing going, with less and less time set aside for evaluating, developing perspective, discontinuing (and, of course, that is the toughest part) and innovating.

This is the very thing I am trying to get at. I think that boards of trustees and boards of regents are going to have to back off from the concept of looking for the man who is well known in Washington or the man who is the mediator and try to start looking for the educational philosopher. I think that is precisely what the American Enterprise Institute is all about, to bring out and air in public the big problems faced in various operations in our society and to involve in all this process the government and the press and all of the other agencies which have a distinct interest in each of these issues. I don't think it's hopeless. But I think that we have to recognize what is happening, I think we have to dig a whole lot deeper. Let me give an illustration.

I recently found myself sitting next to an important corporate executive and he said, "Believe me, I know the pressures you are subject to as a college president, because I am a university trustee." He named a university. And then he said, "Didn't we do a beautiful job of solving our particular campus eruption this last spring?" Instead of expressing my surprise, because I didn't think they did, I asked why he thought the matter had been well handled. He observed that they had calmed things down in a couple of weeks.

Here is a man who had come out of labor negotiations. That had been his life work on the way up to a position of eminence in industry, and his idea of solving the problem was to put a lid on it as fast as possible, giving in on whatever was necessary to calm the thing down.

This is not the way we are going to solve our tough educational problems. We have got to dig down to the roots. Do you or don't you endorse or tolerate a course or an organization which is exclusively black on a campus where you wouldn't tolerate for ten seconds a course or an organization which is exclusively white, that is a tough one.

I think it is only as you have identified the purpose of the institution that you can answer that effectively for that institution. It may turn out to be the opposite decision in another institution with equally valid reasons.

The last thing I did last spring was to send out to all of our returning students and all of the incoming students the full statement of purpose of Rockford College. I observed that there will be tough times ahead of us as on every campus, and I asked the students to spend some considerable time in the summer pondering that set of purposes. If we know what we are trying to accomplish, we will have a firm basis for finding our way through the tough, thorny problems and differences of opinion.

All right. This again is the ideal. You ask, who is attending to these problems. I think that the professional educational theorists are going to be forced to get at some of these things. Actually the survey of professors and administrtors to which I referred has posed very directly some of the problems that we are touching on here. And the American Council on Education had the great good sense to disseminate this study to its membership. The problems are phrased. Part of the difficulty is always in identifying the problem. Now, I am sure many people will be examining and thinking and responding.

I don't think the situation is all that hopeless. I think that the student militants are forcing people to watch the road and map out a course. I think one of the great tragedies is that many universities are responding again in terms of "How do we solve this specific friction that we have with the students?" rather than examining the issues in the larger context: "What is the university here for?" Unless the universities get

back to that question, there are going to be more and
more grievous frictions and confrontations.

JULIUS DUSCHA, Washington Journalism Center:
You seem to be saying that the president manipulates
the board of trustees so he can do what he wants. To
whom is the president of a university responsible?

DR. HOWARD: He is directly responsible to the
board, without any question. But I was suggesting he
is also responsible for them. If the board is ignorant of
the tough issues before the university, I think that igno-
rance is absolutely the president's fault. Some presidents,
finding their life somewhat difficult, have tended to try
to be shields between the trustees and the other constituents of the campus because they know that among
the faculty and the students there will always be people
who will dearly delight in goading the trustees and
shaking them up and giving them a hard time.

But the trustees are grown up. Confrontation is not
anything new to them. If the trustees don't know what
is bugging the students, as well as what they think is
really great about their institution, the trustees simply
can't make good policy judgments.

Soon after I came to Rockford College, I suggested
to the trustees that they serve as hosts to different college personnel in conjunction with their three regular
board meetings. At the fall meeting they invited all
the faculty and the administrative officers and their
husbands and wives (we can do this in a small college)
to a dinner party, where the faculty may choose the

agenda for the evening. At the winter meeting they serve as dinner hosts to 32 student body officers and the students choose the agenda for the evening. And then at the June meeting at the time of reunions the trustees invited alumni to lunch and the alumni chose the topics for discussion.

I must say we went into this program with some trepidation. It has been nine years now. You have no idea what a useful and unifying endeavor this is for the whole institution, to have this kind of interaction. When we face a tough decision—and of course there are plenty of them—I don't try to filter out for the trustees only those views I think they may accept. We bring in the most articulate spokesmen on both sides of the fence, from the student body and the faculty, to speak for themselves to the trustees.

I think the president is responsible for the education of the trustees about the issues, but the trustees are the ones who are going to have to make the final judgment on policy matters.

MR. DUSCHA: About this remark "we bring in," you bring in, you choose the spokesmen who are going to appear?

DR. HOWARD: We ask the dean of the faculty or the chairman of the faculty committee or the student officers most directly involved with the specific issue to choose the spokesman. I don't do this myself.

The more the president tries to steer these things and guide the outcome, the more trouble he is going to have, and so is his institution. I think you have to be honest with your constituencies. And they have to be honest with each other. Believe me, the students and the faculty are not reluctant to say to the trustees what is really on their minds. But that is good, that is not bad.

If I may go back to a previous question a minute, one other thing I wanted to say was I really find little sympathy for the college or university presidents who go around complaining about their jobs. I don't find even fund raising all that great a burden.

Rockford College was committed to build a whole new campus when I came there. They had made the commitment but hadn't started construction. The biggest gift year in the history of our college was, I believe, $167,000. The trustees had decided we should build what they thought would be a $17 million campus. Actually it may approach $35 million. But even the smaller total presents a rather grave differential, $167,-000 and $17 million.

I said, "You know, we are never going to get those buildings built unless we have an exceedingly good educational institution to put into them." So we began very modestly on the construction the first three years, and just raised a little bit of money and built a couple of little tiny buildings.

Meanwhile, we almost doubled the faculty salaries, and went out to hire the people we could afford and when they arrived on campus, they said, "The library collection is impossible. We must have lots and lots of books you don't have, and we must have a first-rate and very costly language laboratory." And the trustees remembering the purposes of the college, said "Okay, great!"

It takes a clear vision of our objectives to direct large amounts of additional funds into the educational program when that enormous construction budget is always with you.

But when there is a truly creative educational program going, then what we have to do to raise funds is go out and talk to people and tell them why what we are doing is important and explain who the guest speaker was yesterday and how he interacted with the students, and what is actually happening on campus. It isn't easy, but I don't think it is all that difficult.

BERTRAND M. HARDING, Office of Economic Opportunity: I would like to pursue this difficult question that you have referred to.

Can you articulate a reasonable objective for an integrated liberal arts college, that might be supported by allowing an all-Negro or all-black organization or class of the sort that you suggest?

DR. HOWARD: I wish I were sure of what the answer to that ought to be.

On our campus we have never had any fraternities or any sororities or any exclusive social agencies of any kind. We have had a significant number of Negroes in our student body for decades. We have, I don't know, 35-40-45 Negroes in a student body of 600 now. Last spring our black students wanted to have a black students organization. But it is a basic policy of Rockford College, dating way back into the nineteenth century, that we have no exclusive organizations on our campus, exclusive on the basis of race, color, religion and so forth. Yet naturally you listen to these requests. The black students do need to develop their self-esteem, and part of that process is understanding and appreciating their own heritage and their own heroes. You can't argue with this. They presented it most persuasively.

One question is, "Does a program in black history and culture get diluted by having white students enrolled in it if they want to take part?" We came to a crunch on this a couple of months ago, and I had to make a decision then. We are still deliberating the policy. But until we get a new one, we stick with the old one.

In the present January Interim offerings at Rockford College we have a program devoted to the literature of the black revolution. And we have one of your staff members (OEO) teaching it who works in our city.

The black students wanted it to be for blacks only. And several faculty members were very sympathetic to their point of view. At the trustee meeting last fall, we discussed this matter at length. We have had a Negro on our board of trustees for some time, and we wanted her evaluation of this issue. She said, "No, we shouldn't permit any separatism because it eventually winds up as condescension and divisiveness."

To repeat, when the question came to me, I held to our policy of no exclusionary anything on the Rockford College campus, pending a review of the policy by our trustees.

Finally, I think again you must figure out, institution by institution, what is at stake, what are the special circumstances and what are the objectives.

Undoubtedly, the fact that we have had black students for as many years as we have makes our circumstances and our ease in interrelationships somewhat different from some other colleges.

KENNETH SPARKS, Office of Economic Opportunity: I have two items I would like you to comment on. First, when you move from a small liberal arts college into one of these huge institutions that we have now, particularly the state institutions, don't you feel that there is a problem with looking to these broad definitions of what a university should do? It seems to me that there is a risk that if you really begin to define what you feel the university ought to do, you maybe begin to limit to an improper degree what the university can do. This is at the larger institutions where state funds are involved and so forth. So isn't there a problem at those large institutions that these definitions or goals tend to be so broad that they really are not very helpful?

Secondly, I wonder if you could expound some more for me on this idea of what you call character education. What kinds of decisions does the president make about what goes into this character education outside of the housekeeping kinds of things like whether girls should be in dormitories and things like that.

DR. HOWARD: First, clearly, as I said before, I think every institutional definition of purpose will be different from every other. I think the statement of purpose of a large unversity is going to be very different from the statement of purpose of a small university. I still can't help feeling, with my prejudices, that even the large metropolitan universities ought to have personal interaction with the students far higher on its list of priorities and written into the statement of purpose. Everybody talks about and writes about the age gap. I have yet to read much of anything sensible about the consequences of it.

We live in a scary world. The bomb is always there. Our cities are erupting in all kinds of violence. Our campuses are wracked with dissension. This is scary. If the young people only talk to each other about the things that frighten them and frustrate them and disappoint them, about how the older generations have messed up this world, then it is no wonder that, as has been recently observed, a significant and growing portion of the brightest students look at the world and see it's hopeless and become hippies and withdraw and smell the flowers; or look at the world and see it's hopeless and become cynics and hedonists and live-it-up-because-what-have-we-got-to-lose; or look at the world and see its hopeless and become the revolutionaries and want to tear it down.

I think the only hope for developing affirmative leadership in this next generation is to have these young people engaged in creative, productive activities with mature people who have lived through wars, who have suffered death in the family, who have surmounted terrible personal reversals and still see hope, some joy, some reason to stand up tall when things get rough. This generation gap is real and growing, and we are paying a terrible price for it. It seems to me that such social phenomena must be thought through and taken into consideration, even in the definition of purpose of a large university.

When the Berkeley thing happened, I read everything I could get my hands on about that uprising. Of all the items I read about it, the one that made the most sense to me was a pair of essays by Max Ways in *Fortune*. He observed that the university in our society has devoted its principal attentions to creating new knowledge. The young people, the undergraduates, have been storing up knowledge, they have abundant energy, and they want to exert leverage on the problems of the real world. Since the university makes no provision 'for the students to do this, then, if somebody stands up and waves a banner and shouts "Peace and Freedom! Follow me!" a number of people are going to do it. Here is the opportunity they have been looking for and sometimes they don't stop to ask themselves whether the would-be leader is honorable or whether he is a charlatan in whatever it is he is proposing.

The eagerness of the students to get involved in the world as well as attending to their studies must be taken into account by the big university as well as by the little one.

The point I cited earlier illustrates what I am trying to get at, the program of Dean Tribus at Dartmouth. I talked to some of his engineering students. They are turned on about what they are doing in connection with their classes. I think there are programs and projects that even the big university can undertake. There is a great wealth of suggestions available from the students if the university will seek them out.

Let's see. Your second question was character education. On our own campus we have it understood that anybody who comes to our campus on legitimate business is our guest and we are the host, and there won't be any picketing or any effort in any way to bother or embarrass, certainly not silence, a guest.

That doesn't mean we expect everybody to agree with him. We always try to have our speakers available for at least an hour after the lecture for a coffee hour with our students so that they can straighten him out, challenge him, ask him more questions. Usually he stays on for lunch.

I don't think that ours is an oppressive community at all. I think it is a very lively academic community where we respect the fact we are there to learn. If we bring somebody there to teach us, we want him to be glad he came, we want to draw out everything he has to tell us, wholly apart from anyone's judgment of the soundess of his views and the validity of his arguments.

I recognize the term, "character education," is in disfavor and one should find a comfortable euphemism. Be that as it may, the point is we believe the university needs to help the students recognize and accept the disciplines and the responsibilities of an academic community and conduct civil discussions even if they think the lecturer is dead wrong.

Let me put it another way. One of the students came in after our Creativity and the Negro Festival, came into my office and he said, "You know, I learned something last week." I said, "That's great, that's why we're here. What was it?" "Well," he said, "I was host to one of the speakers for several days. And it began to dawn on me that I have sort of assumed that anybody who really gets to the top gets there largely as a matter of good luck and good public relations. All of a sudden I am beginning to see that the people who really get there have set a target early in their lives and worked like a dog day and night for years."

I told him if he had really learned that, it might be worth four years of tuition right there.

This is the kind of learning I am talking about. We all take our own pattern of values not from lectures, not from sermons, not from books, mostly, but from other human beings whom we happen to come to respect and admire, and whose judgment we think is pretty good.

DR. ROBERT C. WILLSON, The George Washington University: President Howard, you referred to a specific statement of purpose of Rockford College. Who wrote it? You, a predecessor, the trustees, the faculty, a committee—

DR. HOWARD: It took us 26 months. We had a trustee committee, a faculty committee, an administrative committee, a student committee and alumni committee, all working on their own statements.

They came up with very different answers. These we exchanged and amended and consolidated.

I don't consider it a perfect document. I do consider it a huge improvement over what we had. I believe it is sufficiently explicit to mean something and to be useful as a basis for us to attend to many of the conflicts that arise on a campus.

It was a total institutional undertaking to which we attached a great deal of significance and in which we invested a lot of time.

DR. WILLSON: You have said that it will be very different for a large institution—

DR. HOWARD: Yes.

DR. WILLSON: —than for a small institution.

DR. HOWARD: It has to be.

DR. WILLSON: I wonder then if a president of a larger institution encompassing a medical school and a law school and graduate school and so on will end up following this and perhaps try to run the university by consensus. Having just gone through a little period of consensus, national supposedly (laughter), can a president try to run a university by consensus?

DR. HOWARD: I think he has to make such a judgment quite often. This is what I mean by the president running the university. He has to make the judgment when progress, more progress, will be brought about by consensus and when more progress will be brought about by somebody's making his own judgment and requiring compliance. There will be different times when he will choose different courses and sometimes he will just delay until he has a better idea of which way he ought to go.

But somebody has to make that decision, and I think that somebody is the president.

In a large institution, obviously, he is going to be working, rather than with individual faculty members, with deans and vice presidents and other key officers. I still think the basic mission is the same. The president must be the specialist in the theory of the institution and must enlighten his colleagues on the board of trustees, on the faculty and in the administration about what the theory is and why.

KENNETH GILMORE, *Reader's Digest*: Can you assess a little bit for us how useful you think the rebellion, the protest, on our campuses, whatever you want to call it, has been? Has it served to focus attention on some of the various things you have talked about, the impersonal mass education, the college presidents with 25 posts, the tremendous infusion of government research in the campus. What has been the rebels' contribution?

DR. HOWARD: I do not hold with the theory that the student rebellions around the world are one and the same thing. I think there are very different circumstances provoking rebellion in different places. There may be some common elements, but I don't think the commonalities are dominant.

I think the same thing is true to a lesser degree from institution to institution in this country.

You are aware of the tragedy that occurred today at Swarthmore where the president dropped dead in his office after eight or nine days of siege by the black students there.

It seems to me that an institution like Swarthmore, which has been out in the vanguard trying to jump some decades in our social development, finds it particularly difficult to be under attack by the very people they have been trying to help.

The students don't begin to have the same kind of complaint at Swarthmore that they had at Columbia.

I appeared on a program last summer with one of the student officers of Columbia University and made a point of visiting with him for several hours after the program was over. He asserted that the president of the student body and other officers had tried to get an appointment with the president of the university or the vice president of the university and had been unable to get an appointment for three or four or five months. As I say, this is his assertion.

If it is true, I think that is outrageous. And this would be a very different reason for turmoil on that campus from what happened at Swarthmore.

Clearly the students have called attention to many genuine shortcomings. But if I may return to the Columbia situation for a minute, I think students have also used phony issues.

That boy asserted that the university had heartlessly pre-empted park property that was used primarily by Negroes. It is my understanding that Columbia had checked this out with the Negro leadership in their vicinity who did not feel the university project would seriously harm the park. So that this, I think, was a phony issue.

One of my own concerns about student rebellions is that, one after another, major spokesmen within education and without have praised and applauded student revolutionaries as a main thrust of the speech. You may remember a speech that John Rockefeller gave recently. I think it was entitled "In Praise of Student Revolutionaries," or else that was the headline given to it in the papers.

And I have just come from a meeting of a professional organization where the keynote speaker registered his fear that the student revolutionaries would get discouraged and give up.

We need to rejoice in the fact that the students care and are drawing lots of things to our attention. But I think that as we go down this path of rejoicing about student complaints and student demands, we may do our students a disservice. I think we also need to remind these young people that the history of civilization from a cave man society to whatever level of civilization we may now possess has been the history of the development of institutional restraints.

Had we not developed those institutions of restraint —the law, morality, the family, religion, etc.—we would still be there in the caves clubbing each other over the head.

Every one of these institutions is always going to be imperfect and is always going to need to change and to be improved, but I don't think we ought to encourage people to conclude that we have to tear them all down. I think that we have to realize that these institutions have been built with blood and sweat and tears and giant sacrifice so that people could live together. I think the public commentary on the campus situation this year is badly out of focus on this point.

HOWARD HANDLEMAN, *U. S. News & World Report:* There are many of the students and young people, militants, who say none of our institutions are any good, get rid of them, all of them. How do you go about persuading them that these institutions are of some value?

DR. HOWARD: Sometimes it appears that the people who are assaulting existing institutions don't have anything better to propose in its place. You can point this out to them. The most militant ones, of course, won't listen, or some of the most militant ones won't listen. If you really try and they won't listen, then I don't see any point in trying further.

However, I had two of our professionally disheveled students call upon me in the office before Christmas vacation. They were freshmen and said that they had finally gotten up nerve enough to come in and tell me we had a perfectly terrible college. I asked what was the matter with it. They said we don't have any intellectual challenge.

It turned out that they were not referring to their classes nor to the various speakers and discussions we provide. Rather they were complaining, I think, about the absence of confrontations and headline making, far-out programs. I said, "Ah, I see. We are equating sensationalism with intellectuality. Are you sure that's what you mean?" And we went on discussing this for a while, and then finally I said, "Well, the thing you're going to have to figure out is whether you are at the right campus or the wrong campus. Did you get the statement of purpose which I sent to you before you enrolled last year?" "Yes." "Well, what did you think of it?" "I thought it was for the birds but I didn't think you were serious about it."

(Laughter.)

"Well," I said, "We are."

I think he's going to stay on. But I think you can talk to most of these people if you don't get upset and excited—if you really talk to the issues they raise, and if you talk straight to them. You don't have to pussy-foot.

And the ones who won't talk back, I don't know what you do about them. A lot of them are terribly bright. All you can do is suggest that maybe they aren't listening. Or honestly discover if you aren't listening.

BRUCE ARNOLD, Student Press Association: You set a very strict debate format at the beginning of your speech. I think you are also familiar with the fact that he who asserts must prove. It is, therefore, as I see it, of no import if students, revolutionary students, moderate students can offer no viable alternatives to the present order.

I would like you, if you could, to answer the question just asked a little bit more fully than you have.

It strikes me that it is very curious that you should come across in your formal address in such an authoritarian fashion and then in your remarks afterwards back off and lend a very humanistic, mediating tone. This seems to be in contradiction to the very bold and dashing figure you cut for the presidential role of a university president.

If I were a student and I applied to your college, I hope that over four years that instiution could be subject to some change. From all I can gather, your college—and I hope you won't take this personally, but I suppose it is—is an awfully stagnant place. It seems to me that you have been unusually rigid. I don't know if it is your presentation or what, but you seem to have been extremely unfair in dealing with the student.

I know there are only four of us—or I think there are only four of us in the room, and we haven't spoken out to this point. But many of your thoughts simply send shudders up my back.

DR. HOWARD: Well, it may be my presentation, because I suspect that when you read the transcript of this, you will find there is no contradiction whatever between the illustrations I have offered subsequently and the theory I presented in my speech.

That you will have to discover for yourself, but I suspect this is true.

Whether we have an authoritarian college or a creative college you could only judge by coming to see for yourself. We would be pleased to have you visit us.

I think you will learn that our students think it is a creative place. We have had students involved in the policymaking in the critical deliberations of the college for decades. The student body president has sat on the administrative council for a long time. We have an honor system that dates back to the nineteenth century when Archibald MacLeish's mother was president of the college. The student judicial board determines whether there has been academic cheating, determines whether there have been infractions of whatever social regula-

DISCUSSION   135

tions we have and determines what the penalties shall be, up to the point of suspension or dismissal. If suspension or dismissal is involved, then the student action becomes a recommendation to the president.

I don't know how else to answer what you are saying.

MR. ARNOLD: Well, the first point. You are presenting what is very blatantly a character development education.

DR. HOWARD: Yes! We make no apologies for that.

MR. ARNOLD: Fine. That's perfectly well and good with me. But I want to hear a justification for this institution.

You have asserted a particular philosophy of education.

DR. HOWARD: Yes.

MR. ARNOLD: And that philosophy of education is very much based on the social and economic society we presently exist in. You must justify that.

In addition, how much tolerance and what breadth of freedom does your school offer when you, like a mother hen, bring all of your students together with one non-sensationalistic, quote intellectual—which equates in my mind very much to impotent—person for a pleasant coffee hour after a lecture? Students will not tolerate this, if you do not provide channels for them to express themselves. I grant you that coffee hours are fine. But messages are much more effective perhaps if they are taken to the streets in demonstrations. I'd probably be the one with the first picket sign on your campus, simply to challenge you.

You offer the sweetest target of physical encounter that I have had the opportunity to hear from.

DR. HOWARD: Do you suppose that I am not challenged or that our college is not challenged by students?

Let me just read you the final paragraph of our statement of purpose:

Finally, Rockford College seeks to improve and refine the educational process so that its program will be valid and vital for each generation of students.

Now, whether we do or don't live up to that, again I think you can only judge, not by my pronouncements or tone of voice here, but by seeing the campus for yourself.

Certainly the college is far more authoritarian than many, if not most, institutions in this country. We are not afraid to say, "no."

If we have a policy and it is understood what that is, then it is my job to see that it operates.

Hopefully you don't have to say No and dismiss people. Hopefully you can find out what the problem is. Maybe it is a misunderstanding. Maybe the student or the faculty member or the person from the outside has a valid criticism of what it is we are doing. Maybe our policy is wrong; we are willing to examine that.

But when the thing is clearcut, the buck stops with me and I have to make a judgment.

MR. ARNOLD: And as a student when I come up to you and I say I am enrolled in this institution and I say Your judgment is wrong and I say No, what do you do to me? If I understand you right, what you say is "I am president, I am responsible to the trustees, you're out."

Now, tell me that that offers me the kind of education that will be productive or judge it by whatever other values you want.

DR. HOWARD: It doesn't, clear and simple. We do the best job we can. I think most colleges and universities fail very badly in identifying in advance the precise nature of the institution. If you read the catalogs, they sound pretty much alike. If you read the admissions brochures, they sound pretty much alike.

If you were enrolling in Rockford College, you would have gotten a mass of advance literature week by week from us, including some of my speeches. You would probably read those and decide Rockford is the last place on earth you want to be, which would probably be a good decision for you. Or you might think, "There is a sitting duck! That's the place I want to go and shake up."

We probably have some students who come there with that thought in mind. We have a lot of different reactions to this sort of thing. But we try to make known to the students before they come to us what we are. We send them programs for the festivals we have, we send them a list of all the speakers who have been there in the last four years. We try to make it clear to them what it is they are coming into. This is quite different from many other places. There is a self-selection process in this which I think ought to operate everywhere.

MARVIN REDFIELD, National Aeronautics and Space Administration: It wasn't clear to me in your statements on federally-supported research what the major objection was. You did mention the on-again-off-again aspects of the funding, and the financial plight of the grantee. But was that your main objection to it?

DR. HOWARD: Well, that, coupled with my main thesis, that the research has become of greater concern than what happens to the students.

I think this is an imbalance that has come about in part from a failure to perceive what the purpose of the institution is and in very great part also by the increased volume of federal grants available.

I have been the informal coordinating chairman of a group that started with about 50 college and university presidents who were trying to obtain support for an alternate technique by which the government could make money available to colleges and universities. The technique is a tax credit for gifts to educational institutions.

I presented this in testimony before the Congress back in Mr. Kennedy's time. The proposal is that each taxpayer be permitted a tax credit of, say, $100 which he could send to the college of his choice. Thus, if your net income tax owed is $600, you could, if you wish, send $100 to the local junior college, the state university, Rockford, or Notre Dame, and send the other $500 to Washington.

By this technique each college could spend all such revenues according to its current needs. And the needs of every college are different. Furthermore, there is no overhead. You send us $100 and we send you a receipt which you affix to your tax return. We don't have to pay all those government officers to administer each other to make sure we get and spend the money as Congress specifies. Congress could, of course, divert more or less money directly to the colleges by raising or lowering the tax credit ceiling.

While the powerful universities can be counted on to enlist their full share of such tax credit gifts, the small college would have a better chance than it now does in the competitive lobbying for federal grants. Each college has its own alumni body and its neighbors who may not be able to make big gifts, but most of whom pay at least $100 in income tax, and would be glad to send that first $100 to the college.

Also this plan would tend to put educational funds where the population is. You and I might hope that they would give it to the nearest college to increase the cultural level.

However, many people would give to the nearest college to keep the money in the local economy. "Why send it to Washington where they take a big cut and the rest goes off to Texas or Alaska or somewhere?"

This is a technique which I honestly hope will be given consideration by this administration as a means for getting funds out to the colleges and universities for them to spend as they see fit, in research or lowering tuition, or more scholarships or special programs for black students or whatever they think they need most.

MR. REDFIELD: In that connection what is your expectation as to what the resulting level of research would be compared to what it is now? More or less?

DR. HOWARD: I simply am in no position to judge that. The people in the universities where it is conducted will have to make that estimate.

I do think the decision about how to spend educational funds is better made by each individual campus than it is by a congressional determination that we need a lot of money for this or less money for that, except where Congress needs to make decisions about the research it needs for its purposes, for governmental purposes.

But beyond those, if you are giving out research funds which are in fact intended to be federal aid to education, it is far better to have that volume of money available to the university to make its own decision about how much goes into research and what kind of research.

ROBERT JOHNSTON, Student Press Association: I was wondering if you would comment on the proposal, a kind of opposite side of the coin, that has come from some quarters in the past year. Rather than funneling money in the way you have mentioned or in other ways to colleges and universities, it is suggested, set up loan programs that essentially place full-cost tuition loans in the hands of the students to carry to whatever college they want to attend.

DR. HOWARD: Well, I really don't know enough about this proposal. I am a little uneasy about the tax credit for tuition, I mean when it is a tax credit.

MR. JOHNSTON: This isn't a tax credit.

DR. HOWARD: Yes.

MR. JOHNSTON: It's a loan.

DR. HOWARD: Let me state my objection to the tax credit, because I have given much thought to that. It may or may not apply. You might know better than I. As a partisan I am uneasy about the tax credit for tuition because I think it would tend to put the private college out of business. The colleges and universities, at least the private ones, have to charge all the tuition the traffic can bear. They have no choice, the cost of education is so high. Now, if you enacted a $250 tuition tax credit, the private colleges, I think, would very swiftly add that $250 to the present tuition because they could have all the same students there with the same amount of money out of their pocket.

There is a thrust—again I am not prepared to judge

whether it is good or bad—on the part of many public universities to lower tuition or eliminate it altogether. I think this would tend to spread the two further apart and I think the private institutions would price themselves out of business or just be institutions for the very rich.

I think there is a very good element to this money grant for the student, because that leaves it up to him to decide where he is going to go. It puts the college on its mettle to prove that it is worthy.

Aside from that, I don't know that I have the judgment or have thought it through far enough to comment further.

LOUIS JOUGHIN, Associate Secretary, American Association of University Professors: At one point in discussing the mission of the university you commented to this effect, that in your opinion the trustees should probably have the ultimate responsibility for making the ultimate judgments on the objectives of the educational institution. At approximately the same point in your speech you commented on the fact that education as a process should be responsible, generally speaking, to the public and for the general course of government. The phrase that operations educationally ought to be in harmony, those were the words that struck me. This, I think, might cause some problems. I would like to ask you three specific questions or three elements in one question.

Suppose it is the opinion of the chemists and the chemistry department that the mineral resources of the state are being uneconomically exploited in the interest of entrenched interests, that there has been a failure to recognize new interests.

Suppose at the same time at this unhappy institution the sociologists on the campus have come to the point of believing that the management of the penal institutions in the state are so far behind the times that they are in need of immediate and revolutionary change.

Suppose, finally, that on this same black Friday the students in the institution, or at least the majority of the vocal students, come to the conclusion that, quite apart from the merits of the war in Vietnam, they can no longer tolerate the discriminatory features of the Selective Service Act, discriminatory chiefly in favor of college students.

Now, suppose all these land on your desk on the same day. (Laughter.)

DR. HOWARD: Typical day. (Laughter.)

MR. JOUGHIN: Is it conceivable that any institution could survive beyond the week if the trustees took the responsibility for answering these questions?

DR. HOWARD: Well, I think you are reading into my remarks what I didn't intend.

There is a difference between policy decisions and operating decisions. The trustees' policy decisions are in broad terms about what the objectives are and they may set some limits.

It is hard for me to conceive of any board of trustees which would start making policy determinations about whether the professors of chemistry could register publicly their beef about present utilization of mineral resources in the state. Perhaps some would. But that certainly wasn't what I anticipated in stating what I did.

It seems to me that the kind of things the trustees deal with in policy has to do with whether you are or aren't going to service your students as individual human beings. I do not presume in my statement that the trustees are going to get involved in preventing faculty members from making known their honest decisions. I cannot conceive of that happening at my college or most others.

In terms of the students coming to certain conclusions about Vietnam, please remember I said the trustees are going to have to decide what public issues they do and what public issues they do not take a stand on. This will vary from board to board.

Certainly a board might decide to change its endowment policy, for instance, to reflect current concerns about the Vietnam war. Another board of trustees might very well conclude that its responsibility is to invest the endowment in such a way as to obtain the biggest revenue possible.

This is the kind of thing that I think we are talking about in maintaining individuality among institutions and in turning to the different judgments of different groups of people on tough issues where honest men disagree and where you will have some universities doing one thing and some doing another and some others trying to go down the middle.

SECOND SESSION

DR. ROBERT C. WILLSON, The George Washington University: Professor Franklin, I'm Robert Willson, George Washington University. How did you, who are so much a product of this society and Stanford and Amherst, all controlled by this sinister corporate society, manage to free yourself from all of the indoctrination—(laughter)—of this society and manage to give us this brilliant talk tonight?

DR. FRANKLIN: First of all, I think that what I have said comes right out of American society, and I think similar things are being said by a lot of other people in American society. As far as what happened to me personally to make me radical, I can put my finger on certain things like having to work a lot in factories, working on a tugboat, and so on, that made my class values essentially different from those of a lot of my colleagues.

When I was in the Air Force, as a navigator and squadron intelligence officer in the Strategic Air Command, I began to have my head really turned around. I had gone in as a Stevenson Democrat. And then I found out what was happening. We were at that time concocting stories for the American people that we were under the threat of an imminent nuclear attack from the Soviet Union, when we knew that the Soviet Union did not have a deliverable nuclear system. We were flying bombers over the Soviet Union almost every day. So I said "What's going on here?"

After that, starting to get involved in movement things on a very, very moderate level, just working to help black people secure housing, I started to run into things. When I got into the antiwar movement, a lot happened. I think the processes have been very familiar to quite a few people, realizing where real power is, beginning to understand classes a little bit.

As recently as 1964 I was a precinct captain for Johnson (when I was living in Baltimore). I learned a lot during that campaign.

DR. WILLSON: May I follow up with one other?

I am somewhat disturbed by your picture of society as a whole and the university in particular in the glorious golden past, in which things were ever so much better. This is not my reading of history at all. I didn't find that power was used as democratically perhaps at any time in the past or that it had a broader base and yet, if you didn't exactly say it, that is almost the implication one gets.

DR. FRANKLIN: Oh, no, no, no. I didn't mean to imply that things were better or more democratic or anything like that.

As I pointed out, the medieval university was a feudal institution servicing—

DR. WILLSON: There were marvelous artisans there.

DR. FRANKLIN:—the church and the aristocracy. It was for a very small segment of the society. And certain values were developed in that institution which left a legacy. I certainly don't think that nineteenth century capitalism was any more pleasant than twentieth century monopoly capitalism. In fact, I think that monopoly capitalism provides the physical basis for satisfying all human material needs.

STEPHEN HORN, Brookings Institution: Stephen Horn, Brookings. I guess I should add parenthetically, once a Stanford fund-raising chairman. (Laughter.) I would just like a little clarification. I think that basically what you believe in is really an elitist view of society. It's just that you disagree with the type of elite, because your assumptions don't follow, in this sense: You would say, I suspect, that a university should serve the people, but really only if the people agree with your policy outcomes and positions.

If you took a, quote, representative, unquote, vote of all the people, one man-one vote, and they said the university should support the war in Vietnam or should support something else in society with which you philosophically disagreed, you wouldn't really follow this. In other words, you don't really believe in the democratic representative process. What you believe in is imposing your particular system of values on people, and as long as they agree with that, fine, you'll go along with it.

Now, let me cite you an example from contemporary politics which would show that your cause and effect relationships aren't really quite clear. The prize example is what has happened to the blue-collar worker who is a member of the Democratic party. All you have to do is ask many of the National Democratic chairmen who have worried about this night and day for the last ten years. The guy raised in the thirties who felt economic pressure and moved to the suburbs now has a boat to go to the lake, he gets two cars, he gets the kids in the schools he wants to get them in, he no longer attends Labor Day rallies at Cadillac Square, and is being, in a sense, socialized, in quotes, into a different system of beliefs.

You see, to say that if you admit the blue-collar worker's child in greater numbers into universities he automatically will become this great force for discontent, well, it just hasn't worked out that way. Would you comment on this?

DR. FRANKLIN: Yes. First of all, I don't know where you get the notion of my view as elitist. What I am talking about is relying on the power of the people.

I totally dispute the idea that if the people had made the decision about the Vietnam war that they would have gone into Vietnam. At the time that the ruling elite in this country committed the working class to fight their war, most people in the country didn't even know what Vietnam was, and they certainly wouldn't have voted to go there.

The ruling elite hasn't even permitted a vote to be taken even in its own ruling bodies. It has prevented the one candidate who had even a qualified condemnation of that war from appearing before the people to receive their votes.

What you said about the working class is simply a slightly different wording than what I said people from your class do say about the working class. I said that in the paper and I think that's true because of your class position. If you look around this room, it's very clear. There are no black people in this room. I don't think there are any people from any racial minorities in this room. There are no blue-collar workers in the room.

Now, you talk to Democratic National chairmen. I spend a lot of time with blue-collar factory workers. The ones I know, and the other people in their locals, very strongly oppose the Vietnam war. They certainly at one time did support it out of patriotism and loyalty and so forth, when they believed what the government was telling them. They no longer do.

In many locals there isn't anybody left who supports the war. A friend of mine in the Communication Workers said in his local the thing that turned it around was the guys coming back from Vietnam.

HOWARD HANDLEMAN, *U.S. News & World Report:* I'm a little confused on this, because during your talk you listed *The New York Times* and CBS, I believe, as part of the trustees of Columbia University who are bad. And I submit—

DR. FRANKLIN: Not bad, just rich. (Laughter.)

MR. HANDLEMAN: Well, part of the ruling group. I submit that both *The New York Times* and CBS have been opposed to the Vietnam war.

DR. FRANKLIN: Oh, no, they haven't. They have been in favor of a slightly different strategy for American imperialism in Southeast Asia. At no time has either CBS or *The New York Times* said we ought to get out of Vietnam and given any kind of analysis—

MR. HANDLEMAN: All right. Let me put it this way. *The New York Times* and CBS and many others in this field have presented the raw material on which the workers you talk about have formed their judgments that they don't like the Vietnam war.

DR. FRANKLIN: No. They—

MR. HANDELMAN: You don't accept that?

DR. FRANKLIN: No. It's not that they make a political analysis and go into the Geneva Accords and all of that stuff.

MR. HANDLEMAN: No, no. Of course not.

DR. FRANKLIN: The reason that working people are now opposed to the war is that they are fighting the war. And they understand that and they understand that it is a war that they are being made to fight.

It's very interesting. I was in a cafe in the Mission district in San Francisco, a working class cafe. A bunch of guys were talking, it was right after work, and one guy said, "Boy, if I were in power, I'd use the damn bomb on them; you got the bomb, why not use it? It doesn't make any sense to be in a war and not use this stuff you have. I'd like to get my hands on some of these draft card burners." You know, talking like that.

And then we started talking. In a few minutes what he was saying was in fact that any working class guy in his right mind would not fight in that war, that that very day he had told his 18-year-old son that he would kick him out of the house if he went into the army.

What this guy understood, and he said it, was that working people were fighting the war for the corporations. What got him angry was that the people who had sent him and his people to fight that war had the weapon so that they could win but weren't using it. It was really a very rational analysis. It's not an analysis which said it was an—

MR. HANDLEMAN: Where did he get—

MR. FRANKLIN:—immoral war.

MR. HANDLEMAN:—his basic opinions about the war?

DR. FRANKLIN: From the fact that he could look around and he knew who was fighting the war.

MR. HANDLEMAN: He didn't look at television and he didn't read newspapers.

DR. FRANKLIN: He knew that the sons of his friends were going—were joining the army, that the sons of the people who rule this country were not fighting that war.

MR. HANDLEMAN: Well, if he thought that, he was wrong.

DR. FRANKLIN: Well, what do draft deferments mean for college students?

NATHAN J. MARGOLIN, *U.S. News & World Report:* As a qualified person who has had much contact with blue-collar workers and the lumpen proletariat, I want to point out something. Maybe you can answer it. Workers in this country and in Europe have given up their rights to labor leaders, the hierarchies of labor leaders. Proletarian revolutions have given up to repressive governments, a third class, military officers, professional military officers with labor backgrounds, have been more repressive than other military officers.

What makes you think that these people can run universities?

DR. FRANKLIN: Well, I don't quite understand, first, how you connect what you are saying at the beginning with what you are saying at the end.

I think the Chinese experience is very, very important to understand, in detail, and that in fact we do see in China an example of exactly what I am talking about. Then we get into a big dispute on that question, as on the things that you cited, to begin with about sources of information and what we believe to be true. That's clear.

LAWRENCE SPEISER, American Civil Liberties Union: I'm Lawrence Speiser with the American Civil Liberties Union. A comment and then a question: My recollection of the polls on the war in Vietnam is that they showed that the higher the educational level, the more they were opposed to the war in Vietnam; the lower the educational level, the more they supported it. Now, I would like to ask you if you can, to comment on something that has occurred in the past, principally during the McCarthy period in the fifties. My recollection is that the greatest infringements on academic freedom involving the firing of professors because of affiliation with the Communist party or other organizations or because of their stated views occurred primarily in public universities and not in the private schools in which the board of trustees was chosen generally come from an aristocracy of some kind. In other words those private schools were much more protective of academic freedom.

Assuming my recollection is correct, how do you explain that? Presumably public universities would be more responsive to a voting mass which would include those who are of the working classes, who, it is suggested, are going to provide some kind of democratic control for a university.

DR. FRANKLIN: Okay. There are two things there. First of all, on the working class and polls; the polls, if they say that, are wrong. We have one election to demonstrate that.

In 1966, when the antiwar movement as a whole was not demanding immediate withdrawal from Vietnam but the position was "Stop the bombing and negotiate," Dearborn, Michigan, had on its ballot a resolution demanding the immediate withdrawal of all American troops from Vietnam. Now, Dearborn, Michigan, is almost totally a white, working-class community. Forty-one-point-something percent of the people there voted for immediate withdrawal.

Dearborn, Michigan, in the last election had the same thing on their ballot, and approximately 60 percent of the people voted for immediate withdrawal from Vietnam.

Now, so there is something that—

MR. SPEISER: Well, let me ask—

MR. FRANKLIN: Now let me get—let me talk about the other—

MR. SPEISER: Let me ask—

MR. FRANKLIN: Let me talk about the second point you made.

MR. SPEISER: Let me respond to that one point first, because, as I recall, Dearborn, Michigan, has had a mayor, and a city government, which has been blatantly anti-Negro for years.

Secondly, the bulk, although I'm not sure what percentage, of the support for George Wallace has been blue-collar workers. I wouldn't think you would be interested in placing in their hands the control of a university.

DR. FRANKLIN: If you look at the analysis of the vote in the last election, you will find that the vote for Wallace was directly proportional to income, directly proportional to income and to education.

MR. SPEISER: Well, I'm not sure of that. You mean the higher the—

DR. FRANKLIN: The higher the income and the higher the education, the higher the vote for Wallace.

VOICES: Oh, no. No. No.

DR. FRANKLIN: I have—

A VOICE: What is your source?

DR. FRANKLIN: I'll be glad to bring, when I re-appear here, a citation with a clipping from the news-paper analyzing the election in different neighborhoods with different incomes and different educational levels.

I am aware that the entire propaganda machine that is owned by the class that I said it is owned by said that it was those people "down" there that were sup-porting Wallace. But that turned out not to be true.

Now, as far as the second point that you raise, there is a very, very good reason why public universities are more intolerant on the question of political ideology of professors and so forth than private universities.

The private universities have traditionally felt that it was quite safe for the people who are attending there to hear a few things. But at the public universities it is considerably more dangerous because of the different class background of the students at the public universities. The same people are running those two kinds of institutions. But they understand very clearly how much more dangerous it is for one group of students to hear these ideas than for another group of students to hear these ideas. For the sons and daughters of the ruling class it may be a good idea for them to be exposed to a little bit of that ideology so they can build defenses against it.

FREEMAN HOLMER, Council of State Governments: If what you have just said is true about the same people running the public universities, it seems strangely incongruous that these people, in view of the danger to their interests implicit in expanding enrollments, would be making it infinitely easier for people to attend colleges, as they have been over these past 20 years particularly. If their only purpose in doing this is, as you indicated earlier, to increase the cadre of skilled workers, will they not, now that you have laid out the blueprint for revolution, take the necessary corrective action while they still have control of the mechanism?

DR. FRANKLIN: They don't have any choice.

MR. HOLMER: They have no options open to them?

DR. FRANKLIN: Theoretically they have both options, but it would be much more foolish to destroy the base of highly skilled manpower because of the conjectural premise that that base will produce more political upheaval. You see, as a matter of fact, most people in this room don't believe that argument.

HAROLD ORLANS, Brookings Institution: If the function of radical professors at elite universities is to make sons of the rich and of the existing system more sophisticated and to bolster their defenses, are you objectively serving the interests of the rich or the poor?

DR. FRANKLIN: Who is "you"?

MR. ORLANS: You, in the kind of analysis that you are permitted to conduct at Stanford for the sons of the rich.

DR. FRANKLIN: Well, you see, it's not working out so well right now. (Laughter.) But that's what I'm talking about. Conditions have changed. The private universities are no longer the private universities that they once were. On one hand they are more public because over half their budget comes from public funds. On the other hand, they are more public because they too have a rapidly widening class origin among the student body and among the younger faculty.

MR. ORLANS: How can you have it both ways? How can you be both right in what you are saying now and right in what you said a minute ago?

DR. FRANKLIN: I don't understand the contradiction.

MR. ORLANS: You stated that there was objectively a servile function being served by radical faculty permitted by these elite corporate leaders, tolerated at their ivy league institutions like Stanford; objectively they were debasing the true interests of the intellect and serving the corporate system.

Now, how can you be right about that and yet effective and correct in your argument that you are presenting?

DR. FRANKLIN: Because there is increasingly less toleration. It's clear that somebody with the views that I now have would not be hired at Stanford University.

Even Paul Baran, who, after all, you know, was only a harmless neo-Marxist economist had—(laughter)—his salary frozen for 13 years. They did their best to try to drive him out. And he wasn't an activist.

VOICE: I know some Republicans there that have had their salaries frozen also. (Laughter.)

MARTIN CLANCY, Senate Republican Policy Committee: Martin Clancy. I'm with the Senate Republican Policy Committee. I submit that I don't think you know a hell of a lot about state universities. (Laughter.) You may know a lot about California. I'm from the Middle West, the state university in Wisconsin. You picture the state university as much more subject to witch hunts than private universities. Now, I'll take the university in my own state, the University of Wisconsin—

DR. FRANKLIN: That wasn't my point; that was Mr.—

A VOICE: Speiser.

DR. FRANKLIN: —Speiser's point.

MR.. CLANCY: No, no. Wait a minute. You yourself thereafter said that private universities could tolerate this sort of thing—

DR. FRANKLIN: Yes, right.

MR. CLANCY: —but the state universities couldn't. Well, first of all, the board of regents of the State University of Wisconsin, and many in the Middle West, these invariably include labor leaders, for example, and farm leaders. I don't think you know what you're talking about when you talk about just California and say that is the model for all state universities. I think frequently they are far more open and far more independent and allow far more freedom than you have indicated.

DR. FRANKLIN: Well, the original point was not mine but Mr. Speiser's. I would agree with that point in general. I would acknowledge that there are exceptions to that point.

Generally where the exceptions exist, there is a developed radical movement of one kind or another. At Wisconsin there is still the remnant of a populist movement, and it was able to provide some support for people. That's clear.

MR. CLANCY: But the populist movement you talk of is far removed from what I call the Marxist world view, which you espouse. I don't think that they are even very similar.

SAM ZAGORIA, National Labor Relations Board: I congratulate you on being very provocative. You obviously have provoked a lot of people. (Laughter.) And that was your first objective. I am moved to say something in defense of trustees generally.

You cited Columbia University, and it seems to me that your pointing to *The New York Times* and Columbia Broadcasting System really must be open to some challenge when you consider that perhaps the most critical journal of current journalism is the *Columbia Journal and Review*. I don't know how familiar you are with it. I'm an ex-newspaperman so I read it religiously. It is far ahead of any other criticism of the fourth estate that has come to my attention.

What I am really trying to understand fully is how you would revamp things if you were given all the powers to do so.

At first I got the impression that your objective was sort of a community action operation at the university, the little people, the oppressed, the poor would take over, restructure the curriculum to reflect better their interests and their objectives, that they would be in charge of the administration and so forth.

This is alongside your criticism of the trustees of Columbia and Stanford and other institutions who apparently come from very wealthy backgrounds, have access to tremendous resources and yet have left faculty members in the position where the best paid ones equal that of a beginning policeman. Obviously they haven't done too well in materialistic rewards for the faculty.

DR. FRANKLIN: Historically—

MR. ZAGORIA: You've been at it how many years? Eight years I believe you said? And you haven't reached a par with a first lieutenant of the Air Force. It does

suggest that this system hasn't worked very well. I guess
what I am really coming to is: How would you restructure the univertisy so that more resources would
be available, that your curriculum could be better structured to meet the needs of the people.

DR. FRANKLIN: First of all, the point I was making about the differential in pay was that the best paid
professors are the ones who contribute the most to
profits, to production, and to the ideological and material defense of corporate capitalism; the humanities
professors are on the bottom.

As far as the other point—I guess it was your second
point really, I'm going backwards — about critiques
coming out of the university, that is a very important
function of the university as a manifestation of liberalism, which criticizes in order to reform, patch things
up, keep it going. Certainly the universities fulfill that function very well. That sort of thing would
tend to fall partly in the field of know-how and partly
in the field of ideological knowledge.

MR. ZAGORIA: You can't have it both ways. You
can't on the one hand say that the raison d'être of the
university is to keep people placid and teach them about
the joys—

DR. FRANKLIN: I didn't say that.

MR. ZAGORIA: —of a free economic system and
on the other hand say that an important and useful
part of the university is criticism.

DR. FRANKLIN: Oh, I never said that you keep people placid and joyful. Even within a corporation there are people paid to provide critiques of the way things are going, to suggest improvements. This is entirely within the interests of the power structure; it is in order to keep the system going. That is very different from a radical or revolutionary perspective.

Now, on that other question, about what would I do, I am troubled by it because I think it misses the main thrust of my paper, as did the gentleman's response about a new elite.

You see, I am taking the position that it doesn't make a damn bit of difference really what I am in favor of or what my utopian model is. Remember, I began the paper by rejecting utopian speculation. It doesn't make any difference whether I have this utopian model, you have that utopian model.

MR. ZAGORIA: I'm looking for what you can prove. I'm not looking for utopia.

DR. FRANKLIN: What I'm doing—and this is a classical Marxist way of analyzing things—is to talk about "should" in terms of the processes that are going on at the present. My own loyalties and values I think are clear on what group of people within the society I think should run the universities, which is the question we are dealing with. Now, what in particular they want to do with that university, how they would design it, I don't pretend to know. Which, again, you know, is a classical Marxist approach to the subject. Because anything else—

MR. ZAGORIA: How many courses in Melville do you think there would be?

DR. FRANKLIN: Melville was a proletarian writer. (Laughter.)

MR. ZAGORIA: I'm talking about your kind of humanist courses, if you had that fist-swinging truck driver sitting on the board of trustees or on the faculty.

DR. FRANKLIN: I wish he were. (Laughter.) To do anything different, you see, is, to take my utopian model and say "This is how it should be structured, once you get the power." This would be to do exactly what I was accused of doing and what I refuse to do, which is to have an elitist point of view and say "Here is my model, you accept it, and if you accept it, then I am all for you."

I'm saying, I'm all for you, you take power and run the university—you are going to anyhow—and structure it to fill your needs. I don't know what that new structure will look like in detail.

MR. SPEISER: You have suggested one good model is the Chinese experience.

DR. FRANKLIN: Right.

MR. SPEISER: Are you satisfied with who is running the universities there now, and how are they being run?

DR. FRANKLIN: The workers are running them.

MR. SPEISER: Would there be academic freedom in this set of circumstances? (Laughter.) Collectively, selectively.

DR. FRANKLIN: Yes, there is freedom. The people have the freedom of the universities. (Laughter.) As far as relationships within the university go, they are entirely different kinds of relationships. Instead of passing some tests set up by somebody else to see whether you are going to get on within this system, there are mutual evaluations by the people who are studying. They try to relate what they are doing, and what they can do, to the other people in the society.

MR. SPEISER: But suppose it leaves you as a sitting duck. If I wanted to personalize it, if you had a different point of view, a revolutionary point of view, towards the structure of the university in China, do you think that you would be hired or retained at the university?

DR. FRANKLIN: Look what did happen in China. The Red Guard started denouncing the administration of the universities and putting up big-character posters. They said that these people were running the universities in defiance of the people. Much of what they were saying was very similar to what students in this country are saying. They were attacking the Communist party hierarchy within the administration of the university and they were supported by significant elements of the party itself, including Mao.

MR. SPEISER: But that's a power struggle kind of thing you're talking about. I'm talking about the eccentric individual alone who doesn't represent a power, doesn't have any backing and political pressure behind him, but is suffered by most universities under what might be considered the old fashioned concept that there isn't any substitute for academic freedom or for dissident voices.

DR. FRANKLIN: But, you see, in China the effort is different. It's not that you are *allowed* to have freedom of opinion, but you have a duty, if your opinion is different, to argue for your postion and to try to convince other people of your postion.

MR. SPEISER: Do you really believe that?

DR. FRANKLIN: I certainly do.

MR. SPEISER: Have you been to China?

DR. FRANKLIN: No, but I have—

MR. SPEISER: Have you been to Vietnam?

DR. FRANKLIN: I haven't been to China, I haven't been to Vietnam, but I have very close friends who have been in China, including a close friend who was in the Red Guard for a year at Peking Middle School.

MR. HANDLEMAN: I think you said we must learn and understand what is going on in China in order to look ahead about what is going to come here. I think I may be misquoting you. I'm trying to remember. Is that a reasonable quotation?

DR. FRANKLIN: I don't think it's really a question of—

MR. HANDLEMAN: No, I'm just asking if you said that, if I recall exactly what you said.

DR. FRANKLIN: What I said in the paper was that the fact that a quarter of the world's population has achieved something like the university I was talking about is going to have an increasing impact on radical movements in this country.

MR. HANDLEMAN: Okay. I wanted to get it straight. I'm just asking the question.

DR. FRANKLIN: Whether it will, I think it should.

MR. HANDLEMAN: I wanted the premises of your work.

DR. FRANKLIN: Okay.

MR. HANDLEMAN: What should we learn from the experience in China? Do you believe that the thing, the cultural revolution came from below and that it could have happened if Mao and the power structure there—I think they do have a power structure—if Mao and the power structure had not wanted it? Also, how do you explain in this regard how it was turned on and off at will by order?

DR. FRANKLIN: Well, it wasn't, as far as that goes. It is hard to say, you know, what would have happened if something that was true hadn't been true. Just logically that's difficult. I would say that if it weren't for Mao it would be very doubtful that the cultural revolution would have gone as successfully as it has gone.

MR. HANDLEMAN: —further than that.

DR. FRANKLIN: I think there were deep internal contradictions in what was in fact the power structure. What called forth the revolutionary struggle was the existence of a power structure which people felt had power over them. The party bureaucracy was indeed hardening its postion, beginning to rule as a bureaucracy. So when the students put out the first big-character wall posters, Mao made his own big-character wall poster, which was titled: Bombard the Party Headquarters. Immediately it became necessary for the party headquarters to supply all the materials for anybody who wanted to come in and criticize the party, and to provide walls for people to put up their posters. There was a tremendous struggle that everybody was involved in.

MR. HANDLEMAN: What was the source—

DR. FRANKLIN: This was a movement of the masses.

MR. HANDLEMAN: —of the revolution? Was it a movement of the masses or was it a decision by Mao?

DR. FRANKLIN: Like any movement, it started with a small group of people who were considered very eccentric. It became a movement of the masses. Some movements do and some don't.

MR. HANDLEMAN: Aren't they always taken over by another small group of people? Doesn't history show you that?

DR. FRANKLIN: In China I think the direction is quite the reverse.

MR. MARGOLIN: When you were putting up that somewhat elusive poll—and I might add parenthetically that you seem to share George Wallace's view of the polls as a tool of the Eastern money establishment—I wonder if you could also point out the statistic as to how many students in China achieve higher education and how many students do so in the United States.

Do you favor a majority society making the decision? You say the people should rule. I differed earlier. I think your view basically is only people with the, quote, right, unquote, attitude should rule, not the majority.

DR. FRANKLIN: Those are your words, not mine.

MR. MARGOLIN: Well, do you agree with majority rule? If the people did rule our universities, would you say 51 percent decide it and win and 49 percent lose? Yes, or no?

DR. FRANKLIN: I agree with majority rule.

MR. MARGOLIN: Okay.

DR. FRANKLIN: But I think that I would define majority rule differently from your definition of majority rule.

MR. MARGOLIN: How would you define it?

DR. FRANKLIN: I would say that it is the rule of the majority of the people, not the people deciding which representative of the ruling class they want to misrule them for the next four years.

MR. MARGOLIN: You want a plebiscite, essentially.

DR. FRANKLIN: No, I want organs of people's power, which is why in the movement—

MR. MARGOLIN: Isn't that the same thing?

DR. FRANKLIN: —why in the movement in this country there has been so much stress on participatory democracy, on grass-roots organizing. We want the people to be organized so they have organs of power. Not—

MR. MARGOLIN: Representative organs of power? I mean, isn't this still removed from the direct majority rule in that sense? In other words, you still favor some form of representative government reflecting the views, presumably, of the majority of the people through the majority votes themselves.

DR. FRANKLIN: I'm not so interested in the form of the government. I'm more interested in the content of it.

MR. MARGOLIN: Well, okay. Now, this is where I want to get at you on the form. I think you're copping out when you say you don't want to say how the process should work in making decisions in a university. You know, it's one thing to play around with "Who Should Run the Colleges" but I think you can properly, also, say how they should be run.

DR. FRANKLIN: No. It is very easy to deal with that question because different universities have different sets of organizational rules and somewhat different organizational structures, but they're still basically identical institutions.

MR. MARGOLIN: Who is the university community, let's say, at Stanford? Is it strictly all people that work within the given area of the campus? Is it all people who might someday send their children to Stanford? Is it all the people in the society generally? You've got to face those basic questions and then determine your apparatus.

DR. FRANKLIN: I said very clearly that nobody can run the universities without running society as a whole in America in the last third of the twentieth century.

Now, as for the question about statistics on China, I don't know the percentage of people having what you call "higher" education. One of the things they are doing is integrating the factories with the universities. As I said, there is a rapidly diminishing distinction between students and workers. One statistic I can cite is that prior to the revolution fewer than 10 percent of the people in China could read and write and now almost the entire population is more or less literate. There are vast numbers of people who have only the rudiments of reading and writing, but just about everybody, and certainly all of the younger people, have at least this much now.

MR. MARGOLIN: You don't want to say really in answer to an earlier question what sort of, quote, liberalism, unquote, you would tolerate on the faculty. But I am wondering, if your view of who should rule the university did succeed, do you think you would have room on the faculty for somebody that represented bourgeois society as you apparently would profess to represent anti-bourgeois society?

In your world of the future, would there be room in the Stanford English Department or the Columbia

English Department for one bourgeoisie professor, near the door, maybe a Republican or something? (Laughter.) Or would he be out by majority vote if he voted for the proletariat and not the majority?

DR. FRANKLIN: You keep presenting to me an elitist view and asking me to present an elitist view. Then I am supposed to construct a model of my ideal university. What I am saying is that I don't have a model. I am not engaging in utopian speculations.

I believe that the working people should have the power. Now, when we reach that condition, then, from those concrete circumstances, we can have lots of debates about what that would mean and what would be good for the people. We could talk about legitimacy and justice and creativity and so forth within that concrete situation. For me to take another postion would be to do precisely what you accuse me of doing in the paper.

MR. MARGOLIN: I don't want to force you into a postion but let me ask: Do you think the working people in the world of the future should get rid of academic tenure, which is sort of an old bourgeoisie encrustation on the free processes?

DR. FRANKLIN: No, I myself believe that even now people should not be fired very easily, that there should be rather extreme circumstances involved if someone is to be fired from any job, not just an academic job, that people do indeed in the full sense have a right to work.

Again, in China, to fire anybody is extremely difficult. When the workers in the factory, as part of the cultural revolution, overthrew the management in the factory they could by law not fire those managers. All they could do was to say to them "Look, you sit behind your desk and continue to shuffle your papers but we're going to make the decisions in this factory." They couldn't fire them. I think that was a good thing.

MR. MARGOLIN: They couldn't fire anybody in Nazi Germany either.

DR. HOWARD PENNIMAN, Georgetown University: I wonder if I might help clarify this problem. Maybe I can't but let me try. What you have been doing up to now is really straight out of the thirties. I haven't heard a Marxist or Marxist-Trotskyist line—

DR. FRANKLIN: Trotskyist!

DR. PENNIMAN: Yes, Trotskyist. Yes, Trotskyist line, since the 1930s in the form in which you are doing it. What you are doing is providing yourself a framework within which you put everything that is said into pigeonholes. You defend it with anecdote, not with scientific and evidential material.

When Mr. Speiser offers some information of note, you come up with an anecdote about a worker out in San Francisco or you come up with one very atypical item in Dearborn, Michigan, or you come with an assertion, just a sheer, flat assertion with no basis at all. I refer to the adage that if you are in the humanities you are less well paid than the scientist or the social scientist

—which may well be true. You even know the reason but you have not, as I suspect, any evidence whatever to support it. You might make equally as clear an argument that it was simply supply and demand.

At least some time it would seem to me incumbent upon you to supply the evidence or sometime to defend your statement substantially, instead of with anecdote. Provide the polls that you talk about, provide the electoral material that you talk about. Don't simply drag it out as a flat assertion or as an anecdote.

What I am really suggesting is that you in fact can't defend your postion except as you have this nice rigid, solid world in which you put all these things into one category pigeonhole after another, and you can answer anything.

It is literally true, nobody can debate with you because you've got all these pigeonholes into which you propose to put their points. I suggest that it would be helpful at least if you defended with some kind of evidence the materials you have. Take, for example, Mr. Clancy's problem in Wisconsin. Take your assertion about the scientist and the people who are in the humanities, how they are mistreated "because"—and it is always the "because" which gets you back to the capitalist system and the capitalist leadership and so on. Actually, in the University of Wisconsin there is a provision that any time you raise the level of the top people in the physics department, any department of science, you have to do it right across the board in every other department in the university. So that there isn't you know, this payoff.

Maybe out in Stanford people are living under a very badly paid system and have a much more difficult way of life than most of us in most other universities, but the fact is that in most other universities you wouldn't find this sort of thing that we're discussing.

MR. HORN: It's among the highest paying in the country, Howard. (Laughter.) The sun does shine in California.

DR. PENNIMAN: My sorrow has been misplaced.

MR. HORN: As opposed to the snow in Wisconsin. (Laughter.)

DR. FRANKLIN: First of all, I really would like somebody to deal with the arguments that I have presented, rather than with all kinds of peripheral things because I thought we were talking about—

DR. PENNIMAN: This is, of course, my point.

DR. FRANKLIN: What we were talking about, I thought, was who should run the universities; what is now happening, what are the forces involved, and so forth, to understand what these groups are, and presumably, from our title, to choose sides.

Now, I did not stand up here and lament the impoverished condition of Stanford's professors. Really, I said quite the contrary. I said that I don't think professors of the top universities are working-class people. I took issue with Carl Davidson and the new left analysis of them as what he calls the New Working Class. I said that, on the contrary, I think that professors, particularly in the top universities, are petit bourgeois and somewhat above that position, right?

DR. PENNIMAN: No, because —

DR. FRANKLIN: Okay.

DR. PENNIMAN: —what you said was, the flat assertion was that those who did the work or the business of imperialist capitalists, namely, the people who are not in the humanities where you are in your poorly paid states, were well paid and you, my friend, were getting barely now what you were getting as a first lieutenant when you were in the service—

MR. HORN: Which is nonsense.

DR. PENNIMAN: —which was to suggest that this was the society's estimate of the two. In the first place, well, I don't know. Again I feel sorry for you at Stanford because where we live this would not be true. (Laughter.)

DR. FRANKLIN: I don't know of anybody who seriously disputes what you call the flat assertion that people teaching in the humanities are paid less than other people, that even when—

DR. PENNIMAN: I didn't say—

DR. FRANKLIN: —these are pay scales, everybody knows that the people in the political science departments, the people in business schools, the people in engineering schools, the people in the hard sciences have their pay augmented by consulting fees, by their own contracts—

DR. PENNIMAN: Aaah, aaah, you're cheating.

DR. FRANKLIN: Wait a minute.

DR. PENNIMAN: You're not talking about the universities now.

DR. FRANKLIN: Yes, this is—

DR. PENNIMAN: You're talking about something outside the universities—

DR. FRANKLIN: No, because they get these—

DR. PENNIMAN: —and not the universities themselves.

DR. FRANKLIN: —from the same sources.

DR. PENNIMAN: Aha.

DR. FRANKLIN: And furthermore, they get paid on a different basis. Certainly this is true at Stanford, where they get additional pay for the research that they conduct in the summer. They have constant research funds which are available partly through the university structure and partly through other structures which grow out of the university, as for instance the research institutes connected with the university, as at Johns Hopkins or at Harvard or at Columbia or at Berkeley or at Stanford.

DR. PENNIMAN: And you are excluded from these?

DR. FRANKLIN: From those sources, yes.

KENNETH SPARKS, Office of Economic Opportunity: I would first like to make a comment about some of your sources, which may be a peripheral issue. I found one thing interesting. Immediately after decrying the power of *The New York Times* and the CBS News and the media establishment, you said you were going to bring us in next week the reference to the analysis of the polls; you would bring us in the clip out of the newspapers. This, it seems to me, is just a trifle inconsistent.

But more importantly, you say that the people have not been able to or not willing to debate you on the merits of the proposition that the people should run the university. I think that part of the problem is that when you are asked what the university would be like when the people run the university you immediately cry foul and withdraw.

If we would begin by asking a specific question on how you would stand on specific issues we might get somewhere. When you were asked how you felt about faculty tenure, you were willing to take a position. I take it these would be positions that you would argue for once the quote, people, unquote, would take over the university. Presumably your views reflect those of the people or, at least, you see yourself as one of the people, and that might be a good way to begin. So maybe a good place to start would be on things like some of the safeguards like freedom of speech, some of the basic things that the establishment over the years has held as fairly sacred here.

DR. FRANKLIN: That does seem to me to be a question of what the university ought to be like rather than who should run it. What I mean by people not dealing with the argument is that I haven't heard any-

body come right out and say, "I don't think the working
people should run the university, I think the faculty
should run the university, I think the administration
should run the university, I think such and such a group
should run the university for these reasons."

Instead what I have heard is this indirect attack on
the working class: the working class votes for Wallace,
the working class supports the Vietnam war, etc. And
then my statements are challenged because I don't have
polls right in hand to prove that the working class didn't
vote for Wallace.

MR. SPARKS: No, I would agree. I think that we
have to talk about what a university would be like under
the working class before we can decide whether the
working class ought to run the universities. I think, you
know, you have to draw for us what this university is
going to be like.

DR. FRANKLIN: But, you see, it's a problem—

MR. SPARKS: I'm not arguing that it should or
should not be the working class. I'd just like to know
what the university would be like. What sorts of values
is it going to have? You say that you can't tell us that,
that you are not going to set up a system. Well, it's very
difficult for us to argue with you then.

DR. FRANKLIN: I agree with that and I could
give *my* position, as you suggest, on any number of
issues. You know, I could have answered that question
very truthfully by saying I would defend free speech,

I would defend the right to say everything, and I would. But that doesn't seem to me to be the point.

The reason that we can't talk about this other thing is that there aren't any members of the working class here.

MR. ZAGORIA: May I ask a question? We do have one little example that we can look at. In New York City you had created certain community school districts. One of the things that happened there was that teachers who had taught in the school for many years were told, "Here are your walking papers; we don't want you to report here." Now, these teachers were under the impression that they were protected not only by job tenure but by contracts that were made with the school board of the city of New York. Is this the kind of thing that might happen with, say, working people running a university? Is this a fair parallel?

DR. FRANKLIN: I think that it is safe to say that as this struggle intensifies there are going to be more and more examples of groups of people making demands for power for their own subgroup; for instance, the demand for a black studies department controlled by just black people.

As I tried to indicate toward the end of the paper, what will happen then is that the ruling class will play this group against that, but that tactic will be a self-defeating tactic. One sees this happening at San Francisco State where, you know, almost despite themselves, two parties got into a very close alliance, one party being the Third World Students who a year ago—well, a year ago the black students were hardly having anything to do with the Chicano students there—and the other being the white radical faculty and students. I'd say six months ago the Third World Students were having nothing to do with even the furthest left segments of the faculty at San Francisco State.

Now, those groups are thrown into a very close alliance. Then those groups are attacked by the police Tactical Squad in San Francisco and then the very next day the Tactical Squad attacks the striking nonprofessional workers at Kaiser hospital, the labor council issues a statement denouncing the repressive police tactics being used against both workers and students, saying that the workers stood around and watched the students get beaten up without saying anything and now workers are getting beaten up by the same people, and then the next week police force is used against the workers in the oil refinery strike in Richmond and San Pablo, and those workers begin to make a connection—

MR. ZAGORIA: What has that got to do with the example I cited?

DR. FRANKLIN: So I say, I think that there will be clearly contradictions among different groups of working people. For instance—

MR. ZAGORIA: What would happen at this college you have just been describing?—

DR. FRANKLIN: —the school teachers in New York—

MR. ZAGORIA: —supposing that the people there who were protesting, I don't know the names, had actually gained control of the college and they had said, "Now, we like you, professor, you're a nice fellow and we like the way you lecture but you're not one of us, and so you're out"?

Do you think this would be a more efficient way to run a university than the present efforts?

DR. FRANKLIN: Maybe I can make it easier if I can suggest some kind of transitional demands that could be made that are not utopian, transitional demands I would fully support.

I would fully support, wherever there is a business school, the creation of a school of labor and community organizing where the faculty would be recruited from labor and community organizers, without—

MR. ZAGORIA: You know, in many of your business schools there are courses in labor and—

DR. FRANKLIN: There are courses for that. I would say to begin with, as a transitional demand, there should be equal status for these two. There are places where there is some representation. There are places where there is none.

I would make another demand: That people who work at the university, including blue-collar workers who work at the university, should have a certain amount of time during the day as part of the services that they receive for their labor in which they can enroll in whatever courses they want; and that grading standards for all students be changed, that they be evaluated in quite a different way. That's a transitional demand.

MR. ZAGORIA: These are, you know, very interesting suggestions but actually how do they relate to revising the university?

DR. FRANKLIN: They would cause a radical change in the university.

MR. ZAGORIA: You're talking about opening the doors of the university to an extra effort for working people, to waive prerequisites and to use a no-grading system, let's say, to provide courses that would be of particular interest. But that's not a very drastic change.

DR. FRANKLIN: It is being fought very hard.

MR. ZAGORIA: That's the kind of suggestion that radio and TV people are making to journalism schools: "Look, fellows, we're here to stay. Let's have a course in radio-TV journalism." You're not talking really about a very drastic change.

DR. FRANKLIN: Yes, I think it is. At San Francisco State the Third World—

MR. ZAGORIA: I think you are pulling away from your own broad-scale revision in the whole university structure.

DR. FRANKLIN: The Third World Students at San Francisco State are demanding all Third World Students be admitted to the state college system, regardless of testing. I support that demand.

MR. ZAGORIA: You do. Now, supposing you had a student in your course in Melville—

DR. FRANKLIN: Now, wait a minute.

MR. ZAGORIA: —who couldn't write a grammatical sentence, who couldn't spell.

DR. FRANKLIN: Neither could Melville.

MR. ZAGORIA: But you're the—

DR. FRANKLIN: Melville couldn't spell. Look at Melville's manuscripts. He couldn't spell at all.

MR. ZAGORIA: Would you be happy to—

DR. FRANKLIN: And you see somebody else—

MR. ZAGORIA: —have my sixth grader in your class?

DR. FRANKLIN: No. You see, somebody asked me at dinner time about grammar and the students in high school who are doing radical organizing: "They don't even know grammar. You know, do they really know anything about writing when they're writing?"

The English language produced some of its most eloquent productions before there was a grammar. All of Elizabethan literature was written before there was a grammar of the English language.

MR. ZAGORIA: It seems to me you are arguing no prerequisites for your course.

DR. FRANKLIN: Grammar is a class concept imposed by—

DR. PENNIMAN: There's no merit in training.

MR. ZAGORIA: Sir?

DR. PENNIMAN (To Dr. Franklin): There's no merit in training in your opinion?

DR. FRANKLIN: I think that as far as handling the language, if you want to talk about that—There are many ghetto kids who fail admission tests on English aptitude who are a hell of a lot more eloquent than many of the students we have now with scores on CEEB (College Entrance Examination Board tests) up in the high 600s or 700s; they really can handle the language very ungrammatically, but very effectively.

MR. HORN: Mr. Sparks made a very good suggestion that we try to get you on some of these issues. I think you have a sort of moderate, revisionist view. I see no objection to letting everybody into the university.

DR. FRANKLIN: Trotskyist, revisionist. This is terrible!

MR. HORN: But I think you quickly get down to the tough ones, because one of the basic demands at San Francisco State College is that they have a Black Studies Department limited to black students. Would you favor a White Studies Department limited to white students excluding black? What is the answer to both questions?

DR. FRANKLIN: I think that's a good question, talking about black studies, because I can support that demand as a demand that is coming from those people, even though considered abstractly I don't think that's such a hot idea. Let's say that.

But I support that demand, even though I disagree, because it is coming from the people and I think that they will see the need for other things once they have that. Now, I might be wrong about that. I don't even know if that's of importance. I think the important thing is that those people have power, not whether that Black Studies Department will be what you call "good," considered abstractly.

MR. HORN: Should the blacks have the power to exclude others from taking courses in that department? Should they have the power to decide who should be on the faculty when no other department in the university has that power?

DR. FRANKLIN: All the other departments are controlled by whites. They are merely asking for this one area to be their area, so that they can get themselves together and study their own history. I think that there are problems with that. I do. But I wouldn't even argue with them about it. I would support that demand for now.

MR. HORN: Because it comes from the powerless people?

DR. FRANKLIN: Yes.

MR. HORN: How about a group of white Appalachian poor kids? Could they demand a white studies program?

DR. FRANKLIN: The analogous demand would be a demand for the study of their own people and their own culture and I think that would be a good thing.

THIRD SESSION

DR. HOWARD: I only wish to make one comment in one area. Because the press is here I don't want to leave unresponded to the comments about our festival, with regard to the Negroes and the racial complexion of our college. Rockford College has never had any fraternities or sororities. We have had a significant number of Negro students for many, many years. Last year it was about 8 percent. Now it has become an "in" thing to do to have Negro students and Harvard and Princeton and others who have ignored them for a lot of years are outbidding us with rather extraordinary scholarships. So we didn't have quite such a high percentage in this year's freshman class.

But referring back to the Creativity and the Negro Festival, that was planned in 1964 and held in March of 1965, before Selma, when we weren't all that self-conscious in our dealings among the races. I think we have reached a point now where, whether you do something or don't do something, somebody can make a rational charge that your action is condescending.

Certainly, the educational institutions of this country are in a bind on this point. If they do do anything, it is bound to be condescending in some respects, if one wishes to regard it in that light. It may be many wholesome things, too. But since educational institutions have been what they have been, and this country has been what it has been, any advances you make I think are subject to that charge.

We have, as I think I mentioned before, a Negro trustee. But we also had what I believe was one of the first programs in Asiatic studies, which began in about 1923. I did want to make some comment about the questions on race.

DR. FRANKLIN: Yes, I have responses on a few points. First of all, of course, I am not against power. That would be ridiculous. It's a question of power for whom. And I am for, as I think I made very clear, power for the people who are presently without power and who are in a position of being exploited and/or oppressed.

In this, I am not, as suggested, somebody who advocates a high concentration of centralized power. Quite the reverse. I think the Chinese experience has been very, very important there. I refer you, for a very interesting article, to Barry Richman, January-February, 1967, *Harvard Business Review*. He is chairman of the Management Theory and Industrial Relations Divisions of the Graduate School of Business Administration, UCLA. He discusses decentralized decision making in China, grass-roots decision making.

As I have mentioned in my paper, I think one of the most important things about the movement in this country is its concentration on participatory democracy and building grass-roots organs of power. I am for power to the Soviets rather than power to the party. In my own experience here I am very much influenced by the unions that I have been in, and having been in only one that was a good union. That was on the tugboats. The reason that was a good union was that every union officer worked on the tugs and was directly responsible—physically responsible—to the people he was representing.

Now, about the question of who should be on the governing boards. Dr. Howard uses the expression "successful people." I think that is a rather tautological term. The question is: successful at what? I don't think that the highest achievement of mankind is being successful in business. I think there are many other kinds of human success that are much more important in directing educational decision making.

The other misconception is to think that I would be saying that all poor people are good and all rich people are bad. That's preposterous. It's not a question of being ethically good or ethically bad as an individual; it's a question of the needs of the people. For example, the Rockefellers, I believe, own, in various ways, 60 percent of the arable land in Venezuela. And people in Venezuela are starving. Nelson Rockefeller may be a very nice man who is very kind and so forth in his personal relations, of a high standard of personal ethical behavior. But objectively he is playing a very bad role, considering the needs of those people in Venezuela. I think the people in Venezuela should have power over their resources.

A very interesting question is this one about working people picking what novels should be taught. Dr. Howard seems to think it unthinkable for me to be affirming that their judgment would be an important judgment, or a judgment which should carry more weight than the judgment of academic critics. But that is in fact the position that I maintain. I think it would be a very long discussion indeed to try to define what we mean by, let's say a "good novel." Good for what, good for whom? I think that it has been very clear that the push within the educational system as a whole, not only in universities and colleges but way down, has been a push in the direction of this dominant culture of ruling ideology. This suggests that that which is good is that which is complex, which has a very intricate structure, which is difficult to understand. "Simple" has become virtually a synonym for "bad."

HOLMES ALEXANDER, McNaught Syndicate columnist: I'm just wondering, sitting here. Do you think we have a right to wonder whether, as well as you speak, as forcefully as you put your arguments, that we are not listening to subversion and therefore should resist it, subversion for the overthrow of what we have in favor of the foreign policy of an avowed enemy? Do you think that is a reasonable reaction that a man would have sitting here listening to what you say?

DR. FRANKLIN: Oh, I certainly think my arguments are subversive, no question about it.

MR. ALEXANDER: Well, should not we resist them, then?

DR. FRANKLIN: Well, it depends on who you are, you see. I mean if you are in a position of having power and having wealth, well, certainly you should resist the arguments, I suppose, and perhaps you will. But the argument is an argument, just to put it in its simplest terms, that the people, the majority of people, working people, should have control over all their resources, including the educational resources. Now, that is an argument which is opposed to certain parties' interest.

If this is an enemy argument, an argument of a foreign power, I don't comprehend the term "enemy." It is an argument for the American people.

MR. ALEXANDER: There is a foreign power that wants to overthrow us. You are quoting their line. I think you would expect us to be a little resistant.

DR. FRANKLIN: You have an image in your head which lots of people have in their heads, that some foreign power is going to overthrow "us," and seize our country. But that's preposterous. Are the Vietnamese going to come and invade our country? Are the Chinese going to come and invade our country? This is absurd.

We're talking about ideological arguments, in which some people are saying that one system is good and some people are saying that another system is good. One side of the argument is saying that the working people should have power and the other side—and I am glad it has come out clearly now—is saying that those with wealth and power should have the power. Which is simply a rephrasing of what I said in my paper last week.

MR. ALEXANDER: The record is that when we don't keep our defenses up the Soviet Union advances westward through Europe, and it has come as far west as Alaska in history. So I don't see how you can expect us to be docile about that.

DR. FRANKLIN: I think it is better to put it the other way around, to see the expansion of American imperialism as it took a continent away from the Indians and the Mexicans and advanced throughout the rest of the world, seizing as much territory as it possibly could, for the benefit principally of one small group within society.

MR. ALEXANDER: Isn't that the law of life and nations?

DR. FRANKLIN: No, I don't think so.

MARTIN CLANCY, Senate Republican Policy Committee: You made a comment at the beginning of your speech tonight, Bruce, that most of the audience's objections last time were peripheral, etc., and that they were unable, as it were, or did not choose, to meet your arguments. I would include my objection, which was that I didn't think you knew what you were talking about in your analysis of, for example, who runs universities and what their board of regents is made up of and so on.

I think your comment is correct, but it is correct for this reason. You have a theory of history and man and society; you have laid all the facts from the rack of the world on it like a procrustean bed; you have cut off a head at the top of that one fact and a foot over here and an elbow over here and an arm over here, to fit everything in it. My objection—and I cited the University of Wisconsin as contrary to the way you describe a board of regents—is that the Wisconsin board of regents nevertheless fits into the society as we see it, in what we consider to be part of the debate, as it were, on "Who Should Run the Universities?" It is in the context of the society that we live in and which we believe in. I have no doubt that would never even approach your ideology. So the fact that these comments were peripheral was because you were running right by us, as it were.

Take, for example, your concept of the medieval university last time, for the aristocracy and the Church. You're not correct in that. If you have studied anything about medieval universities, that wouldn't be a correct description of what went on there, of why radicalism prevailed there and so on. The aristocrats were all out fighting. Very few aristocrats attended any medieval universities. These little facts, as you go along, to my mind emphasize almost the impossibility of this debate, from your viewpoint and from our viewpoint. I'm talking about this entire audience, regardless of party affiliations, liberal, conservative, and so on. I don't see how we debate, unless we simply want to debate a basic theory of society, with one part the history of man as against your theory.

DR. FRANKLIN: Okay. You say that I don't know what I'm talking about because I say that boards of trustees and regents are overwhelmingly made up of big businessmen. I think that you don't know what you are talking about if you disagree with that. I think Dr. Howard very much agrees with my position and said in his rebuttal that if I thought that boards of trustees and regents were liberal, I didn't know them. I refer you—

MR. CLANCY: I didn't say they were liberal.

DR. FRANKLIN: —for concrete evidence to the survey, released last week by the Educational Testing Service, on who is on boards of trustees and regents, what their position is in society, and what they think about a number of things. On the second point of fact about the medieval university, what I said was that it was attended by a very small segment of the society and that it serviced the needs of the aristocracy and the Church.

MR. CLANCY: It certainly serviced the needs of the Church for a while. But when you say it served the needs of the aristocracy, I insist you are not correct, historically.

DR. FRANKLIN: Well, surely, Mr. Clancy, you are not suggesting that the medieval university was a university that was wide open to masses of people, I mean you would agree that it was a university open only to a very small elite in the society.

MR. CLANCY: No. Very poor young men went to these universities, picked their teachers, cheered them on, fought other students, etc. Pretty wild places they were.

DR. FRANKLIN: What percentage of the society was enrolled in the universities?

MR. CLANCY: That's not the point. You're talking about the makeup, and you say no poor person could go there. I say frequently and very generally they could. Now, this is just one of the facts that I think you have mutilated to fit it into your theory of history.

DR. FRANKLIN: A very small percentage of the population could even read and write at that time.

MR. CLANCY: That didn't mean they couldn't go to the university. Do you think they had entrance exams?

DR. FRANKLIN: You had to be able to speak Latin in order to be at a medieval university, and read it, in addition to your native language.

MR. CLANCY: No, you did not have to read Latin. But anyway—All right. I still insist that I bring in histories of various medieval universities and show that your concept is not correct. In other words, I think you have mutilated that, in part, because you have to fit everything into this procrustean bed of yours.

STEPHEN HORN, Brookings Institution: I just want to add a footnote to Martin's argument. Your answer, Professor Franklin, to him, if you follow that consistently, has just destroyed your argument on the value of Chinese universities, because you asked the question "What percentage of society attended them?" That is the question I asked you last week in terms of China.

DR. FRANKLIN: Yes. And I answered that last week by pointing out that the distinction between university and factory is rapidly breaking down because everybody is both studying and working, so that a vast percentage of the population is engaged in what we would call "higher education." The institutions are being reshaped very, very rapidly. I can't give you statistics on that. I don't think anybody could give you statistics on it. But as far as who is going to the universities and who is making the decision about who should go there, what the course content is in the university, and how evaluation of students is conducted in the university, I think that is all readily available information.

JAMES GALLAGHER, Committee on Un-American Activities: (Laughter; applause.) I was here last Thursday and held my hand up for quite a while but Mr. Franklin was very busy. (Laughter.) I would like to preface my question to him tonight with something that happened to me on the way home. I live over in Virginia, I have to cross the 14th Street Bridge, and it was a miserable night, if you will recall. I haven't learned to swim across the river yet, even though I have mastered Mao Tse-tung's little red book which allowed him to swim 40-odd miles down the Yangtze. But I still drive my Volkswagen over the river, and on the bridge a car had stopped prematurely and a truck driver who was behind that man did a very able job of avoiding the car in front. On the rest of the way home I recalled a statement made, I think perhaps by the Brookings man here, about the working class taking over the university, when reference was made to a truck driver.

So during the course of my drive home I thought "That was a very able truck driver who avoided a near collision on the 14th Street bridge, but wouldn't it be a shame if Mr. Franklin were at Georgetown University Medical School and this same truck driver were handling the heart transplant and handling the scalpel. He might perhaps end up with my liver. (Laughter.)

I noted, Mr. Franklin, you wrote an article in PL, *Progressive Labor Party*, called "Lenin, Youth and Revolution," whereby you are plugging a book that just came out of Moscow by Lenin on youth. Your lead line here is:

As revolutionary ferment spreads and deepens on America's campuses, help suddenly comes from a rather unexpected source—Moscow. *Lenin on Youth*, a new volume in Progress Publishers' series of selections from Lenin, could be a powerful weapon in the struggle for a socialist America. [I note you didn't say university.] It should be carefully studied by every revolutionary American student and young worker.

And you conclude with this passage:

In probing deeper into this familiar situation, Lenin reveals what pulses there—the stirrings of a revolution." "The beginning of a mass student struggle" does not indicate the isolation of students. Quite the reverse, it "is a political symptom, a symptom of the whole present situation." The first ones to recognize this, then as now [1903], are not the students but the authorities. They are the ones who know what is at stake—their very survival.
Decades of experience have taught—[Now you are quoting Lenin, I assume; you don't say that, but it's small print.] have taught the government that they are surrounded by flammable material and that a mere spark, a mere protest may start a conflagration.

Then you continue:

> The conflagration has already started on the campuses as well as in the cities and even on the farms of the United States. To fan that conflagration is now the task of a revolutionary party.
>
> *Lenin on Youth* gives to that revolutionary party the help of somebody who has been there. Read it.

I submit, Mr. Franklin, are you genuinely concerned about who should run the colleges or who should run the country?

DR. FRANKLIN: As I pointed out last week, Mr. Gallagher, it is impossible at this point, because of the interpenetration of the universities and the other major institutions of the society, for anybody to run the universities without running the whole society. That's a quote.

DR. HOWARD: May I just make one comment to which someone might want to respond? Professor Franklin said that we had finally made it clear that we are talking about a confrontation between the poor on the one hand and the powerful on the other. If you are representing my point of view as the powerful, I would like to disagree. My position is, in contrast to having one class of the society running it, the poor, we should have an open society where everybody has a chance. And this is different.

HERMAN PIRCHNER, Associated Student Governments: I wanted to address this to Dr. Franklin.

Last week when you were describing the evolution of your philosophy you mentioned you entered the Air Force as a Stevenson Democrat. Since then you have admitted to being a radical and a revolutionary, though you have never pinpointed any organizational allegiances you might have. I am sure that you are aware Chairman Mao has said, and I quote, "We Communists never conceal our political views."

So in keeping with the spirit of Mao, I would like to ask you if you are currently affiliated with any political activist organization and also what your association is with the working class you continually refer to.

DR. FRANKLIN: Yes. As far as my own ideology, I think I have made that very clear; I used the word Communist in referring to myself tonight. I would consider myself a Communist, a revolutionary, a Marxist Leninist. I am not at present, nor have I ever been—(laughter)—affiliated with any political party except the Democratic party and the Peace and Freedom party, which is hardly a revolutionary party. The reason is that I think that the American Communist party is really not a revolutionary party, and there are extreme problems in the other parties which have a better line than the American Communist party. I don't think that they have the potential to be an American revolutionary party, although I might be wrong about that.

The other part of the question was relationship—

MR. PIRCHNER: To the working class.

DR. FRANKLIN: —with the working class?

MR. PIRCHNER: Let me just refer back. Do you mean you have never found a group which suits your goals? You don't participate in any organized activity to find the type of thing you seek?

DR. FRANKLIN: Oh, we have a group on the Peninsula called the Peninsula Red Guard— (laughter) —which you probably haven't heard of, which I am a member of. That's not a political party.

The other question was the relationship with the working class.

MR. PIRCHNER: That's correct.

DR. FRANKLIN: You mean right now.

MR. PIRCHNER: That's correct.

DR. FRANKLIN: Well, right now I teach at Stanford. Now, as I indicated last week, there is a big debate inside the left as to whether university teachers are members of the working class or not. I'm not entirely sure about that. That's difficult. (Laughter.) I spend a lot of time—I would say practically all my social and political time—with working people, people we would all recognize as working people, blue-collar workers.

HAROLD ORLANS, Brookings Institution: First I would just like to express my personal discomfort at the personal character of some questions which I think were inappropriate to an essentially intellectual discussion. I recognize the difficulty of conducting a serious intellectual discussion with Dr. Franklin, whom I regard as an idealogue who would be incapable of meeting the first and reasonable test that should be put to any serious and genuine intellectual. That is that he be able himself to cite the evidence which he would accept to negate his theory, to disprove it, in short; that he be prepared to consider facts, both pro and con. This is the test which Darwin applied. I submit that the record of Dr. Franklin's discussion has shown that he is incapable of recognizing any fact, or himself even positing it, which could possibly show any element of his ideas to be wrong, because either it supports his position or it demonstrates the opposite, which through some Hegelianism is converted into proof. And so, to my mind, he is an idealogue.

But I would like to ask two factual questions which I think it is fair to ask you. There have been repeated questions here about the capacity of workers to set the curriculum, which you have answered only in English. I think you have ducked the hard questions.

Would you please indicate if you believe the working class is qualified to set the curriculum in, for example, physics, genetics, medicine, and engineering? And if so, what might be a proletarian law of relativity or a proletarian law of genetics. I think they tried it, rather unsuccessfully.

My second question is again a very simple one: What percent of the American population do you regard as being members of the working class?

DR. FRANKLIN: The areas you cite are the areas that I refer to in my initial paper as the kind of knowledge that I call useful knowledge or know-how. Now, here, you see, I would agree with Dr. Howard that the question is: To what uses is that knowledge going to be put?

Clearly, in the field of medicine, we have distinctions between present decision making and what decision making would be if the people with the greatest needs for medicine were in fact in control of the medical school.

There are many contradictions in the medical schools at universities. But in general I think it is safe to say that the emphasis is on curative rather than preventive medicine, and one of the characteristics of socialist economies is a shift to emphasis on preventive medicine, with particular stress on developing clinic personnel.

As to things that I would advocate if in fact the working people had control of the schools of medicine, I would propose that anybody who goes to the school of medicine to learn to be a doctor be paid to be a student and that, on the other hand, he not have the prospect of enriching himself at the expense of people who are suffering from disease.

MR. ORLANS: But you are talking of the social structure of medicine, not of its scientific character.

DR. FRANKLIN: Well, you see, I don't think that people understood the distinction I made in the paper. There is one kind of knowledge that is useful knowledge, know-how, which I said can belong to anybody, to one social class or to another social class, one can use it or another can use it. That, I said, is different from cultural knowledge and ideological knowledge, which can only be used by the class that produced it.

MR. ORLANS: Is the working class qualified to teach physics?

DR. FRANKLIN: No. In order to—

MR. ORLANS: Qualified to determine what should be taught in a physics course?

DR. FRANKLIN: No, not in detail. You see, there are two different questions. In one case, that is, the second case, cultural knowledge and ideological knowledge, key decisions are decisions about curriculum and decisions about who is going to be doing the teaching. In the other area, the area of useful knowledge, the key decision concerns the use to which this knowledge should be put, not the content of the course or who is teaching the course.

Of course, in that area you have to be a physicist to teach physics. Nobody would argue with that. That's a very different thing from the example Dr. Howard cited of a novel.

DR. HOWARD: I also cited an atomic physicist. So I had missed your original distinction, as this gentleman has.

DR. FRANKLIN: You see, in the case of a novel I do not concede that an academic critic who publishes things about the architectonic structure of *Finnegan's*

Wake is a better teacher of literature than, say, somebody who is going to go in there and teach science fiction from the point of view of somebody who has just been very interested in science fiction and read a lot of it, so that it has affected his life and he thinks that it is of interest and significance for other people.

MR. ORLANS: Would you acknowledge that in the areas of useful knowledge the working class must sit at the feet of the scientists and engineers?

DR. FRANKLIN: No, I don't think it is a question of sitting at their feet. I think that teachers are servants of the people, not the reverse. The teacher gives his knowledge to other people. And I don't think that in order to do that a servile situation should be created. I don't think that the way a classroom is set up is a good way to set up a classroom. I try to set up my own classroom differently.

MR. ORLANS: If you are graduating engineers— we are talking of a Communist society now, not of America—to whom are you going to give responsibility for building bridges over which proletarian army vehicles will travel? (Laughter.) You want to certify that that bridge will stand and not fail the people's army. Whom are you going to permit the authority to certify that these engineers are qualified to build those bridges?

DR. FRANKLIN: I think that the only authority that governs qualification for bridge building is an empirical authority. That's how we measure whether somebody knows how to build bridges or not, whether they fall down or stay there.

VOICES: Ohhh. (Laughter.)

DR. FRANKLIN: We don't first test it and then say "Here, go build the bridge," of course. But that is the test, it is not an "authority" who says, "Well, this fellow is obviously a bridge builder." You know, that is an unfortunate example for your case because there are lots of working people who would be very good at giving courses in bridge building.

MR. ORLANS: Well, so that I may stop hogging the floor, would you kindly answer the second question: What percent of the population do you regard as working classes?

DR. FRANKLIN: I don't have a percentage. If you pushed me to the wall and said "Name a figure," I guess I would say something like 80 percent. (Laughter.)

DR. HOWARD PENNIMAN, Georgetown University: Could you define it now? We're back to that one. We've been trying for two weeks to get that definition.

DR. FRANKLIN: You want me to define social classes?

DR. PENNIMAN: Well, I want—

A VOICE: No. That 80 percent.

DR. PENNIMAN: —these workers defined so I know who that 80 percent is.

DR. FRANKLIN: A worker, a member of the working class, is somebody whose only way to subsist is to sell his labor to somebody else, who in one way or another has ownership or control over the means of production.

DR. PENNIMAN: So you include teachers in that category in the United States?

DR. FRANKLIN: I went through a long thing last week about the problem with teachers, particularly in a university. You have people teaching in a business school who are in fact businessmen. You've got people teaching in a law school who are really corporate lawyers, more than or as much as they are teachers. You have people in several fields of science and engineering who are independent contractors with the Department of Defense; they have research teams that they hire themselves; they hire and fire.

Now, those people obviously are in a very different class situation from the humanist scholar, the bohemian writer who is teaching a writing course or, for that matter, from most history professors. But even in a department like history you have a distinction between those people who are heavily funded from the government or some other richly-endowed source on an ongoing basis and those people who are primarily publishing in learned journals and not funded in that way.

DR. PENNIMAN: People who publish in learned journals are workers? I'm just trying to—

DR. FRANKLIN: No. I said last week in the universities I think that university teachers are in general what you would call petit bourgeois, if you want to use the classical term. Although I can see a lot of weight in the argument made by people like Carl Davidson and Jim O'Connor that teachers are in fact members of what they call the New Working Class. I certainly want to make one thing clear. I do not think that the distinction between workers and other classes depends on whether you wear a blue collar or a white collar.

DR. PENNIMAN: Or whether you own stock or don't own stock.

DR. FRANKLIN: Well, if you own enough stock so that you are subsisting to some extent on the income from that stock, or the profits from buying and selling that stock, then to a certain extent you would be part of an owning class, in a small way or a larger way.

A class analysis of society is not a bunch of baskets that you throw people into. It's a way of going at society to understand the forces that work within it, how these forces are changing, their internal relationships and their relationships with each other. Surely we all make classifications. We don't look at a society as just a collection of individuals: There is one and there's another and there's another and they are each unique. We recognize that they are each unique. We know that from our own experience in the world. But we also know that it is necessary to have conceptions of the operating groups in the society, if we want to understand how the society works.

DR. ROBERT C. WILLSON, The George Washington University: President Howard, I am afraid you might get off the hook, so I want to get this in quickly. I would be an advocate of faculty power if I hadn't attended so many faculty meetings. (Laughter.) But having attended them and having heard both of you gentlemen, I am not in favor of either of you. (Laughter.)

President Howard, you spoke of the competition among our institutions of higher learning as having bred or having produced all of our goodies. Now, I admit we do have a lot of goodies and I am very happy that we do. But I don't see how this gets back to your fount of all good things: that university, that board of trustees.

I don't believe that the boards of trustees around the country, through their agents, maybe even the presidents, have produced this competition. I suggest to you that it has been the faculties, perhaps which have been put together by money raised through these people occasionally, that have done it. The real progress that has been made has been made by the faculties and not by boards of trustees trying to outdo each other in intellectual or technical achievements.

DR. HOWARD: I am a little confused about the basis of your assumption or the interpretation of what I said. I think in referring to Carleton, Reed, and

Swarthmore, I was referring to the productivity of the faculty, not the board of trustees.

DR. WILLSON: But your original statement was that all of the guiding power of the institution should come from the board of trustees which acts through the president.

DR. HOWARD: No, I don't think that was my original statement. I think what I assigned to the board of trustees was broad policies and then I said—

DR. WILLSON: A commitment to excellence, in every catalog in the university—in the country.

DR. HOWARD: —and what I said was that within the broad framework, the policy framework of what that institution is, it is the faculty that must have the decision-making power. I think you will find that in the original text: The decision-making power about the academic and research functions on campus.

DR. WILLSON: Beyond that commitment to excellence, which we all know is in every institution's catalog or brochure—

DR. HOWARD: It isn't enough.

DR. WILLSON: What is this thing that is going to be done? You said in your first appearance here that that marvelous statement of purpose which was worked over for so long was put together by a great big committee, that this basic document was not put together by the board of trustees of your college.

DR. HOWARD: No, it wasn't. Indeed, none of the policies of our college, I hope, are determined simply by unenlightened trustee deliberation. We go quite to the opposite extreme in turning ourselves inside out to present from all of the internal constituencies of the college the opposing views on any policy issue but the decision on a policy issue rests with the trustees. We hope it isn't an uninformed decision.

MARJORIE ZAGORIA, student: My name is Marjorie Zagoria and my affiliation is just a student, rather interested and peaceful, and I'd like to direct my question to Dr. Howard. When you mention the destructive forces of the students and the sit-ins that disrupted their schools, I wonder, isn't it a possibility that these students, rather than trying to be destructive in their schools, see knowledge as rather a kinetic and a changing thing? They want to broaden the scope of knowledge and the courses presented at their campuses. So that theirs is not really a destructive force but really an instructive and a constructive force?

DR. HOWARD: Going back to the other discussion, I don't think I attributed evil motives to most of the student activists. On the contrary, the student activists have been most helpful in identifying, on many campuses, real problems that ought to be attended to and also in drawing to the attention of the institution and of the public many things which ought to be attended to, which aren't even recognized as problems, but things the institutions ought to do.

My concern is the techniques by which change is undertaken and the impact upon the educational institution of coercive techniques. For instance, I spent several hours talking to a student leader who had been leading a highly-publicized, activist effort. He identified himself as the vice president of the student government and he said that for six months he and the student body president had been trying to get an appointment with the university president or the university vice president but were unable for six months to get an appointment.

Well, this is not to be tolerated. That's outrageous. And so they led a fracas. I asked him if he had called any of the trustees. He said no. I said my guess is that if you had simply called the secretary of any of the trustees and made a simple statement of who you were and what this problem was that something would have happened in a hurry. I believe that. And if that was the real basis for that huge mess on that campus, that's idiotic.

BERTRAND M. HARDING, Office of Economic Opportunity: I'd like to return to the more interesting subject of attacking Dr. Franklin. (Laughter.)

DR. HOWARD: I don't know whether to be complimented or insulted. (Laughter.)

MR. HARDING: I think, Dr. Franklin, that the thing that perhaps put you at odds with this middle-class, waspish sort of audience that you've got is the lack of morality in some of your argumentations. I cite as a prime example of it what you did when you stated that Dr. Howard gives it all away when he names the first qualification of his ideal president and then go on with his quotation. Now, I happened to have heard Dr. Howard. My recollection of his remarks, although I do not have a copy of them, was quite to the contrary. This was not his idea of an ideal college president at all but quite to the contrary.

DR. FRANKLIN: That's a very serious charge and—

MR. HARDING: I intended it to be. (Laughter.)

DR. FRANKLIN: I would like to look at Dr. Howard's text. I think that I can demonstrate that I did not misrepresent his argument, but perhaps Dr. Howard could comment on that—

MR. HARDING: Maybe Dr. Howard—

DR. FRANKLIN: —while I'm looking for that particular quotation.

MR. HARDING: Maybe I misinterpreted from memory Dr. Howard's view that he was not plugging for the college president to get appointed to the National Science Foundation, the presidential task force, etc., etc.

DR. HOWARD: As far as I was concerned, that was not an ideal president.

MR. HARDING: That's exactly what I recall.

DR. HOWARD: But I may have used that term in talking about the ideal—I don't know but I certainly presupposed that the best president would be one who was a comprehensivist and whose main function was dealing with the theory and the purpose of the institution.

MR. HARDING: As you can have an ideal that does not reflect the present situation, I agree with your analysis of what the president's qualifications are and I am sure that Dr. Franklin agrees. That was not your objective in your presentation—

DR. HOWARD: Oh, that's right. I thought he turned it upside down.

MR. HARDING: He did turn it exactly upside down.

DR. FRANKLIN: Yes, it's on page 27 of the original text and I believe that I may in fact have misunderstood Dr. Howard's point. I would like to read the passage preceding the one in question:

> I believe it is essential that the man who holds that office be a highly capable scholar whose particular academic capacity is as a comprehensivist. But before elaborating on what ought to be the talents of the president, it is useful to register upon present circumstances and how they have skewed the work and the concept of the university president.

The passage that I quoted immediately followed that, and I see that taking that without its ironic tone is a misinterpretation of Dr. Howard's remarks.

I do think, however, sir, that your use of the term immoral there is not correct at all; as you can see, the context is a difficult context.

MR. HARDING: You think it was an error rather than an intentional perversion of the doctor's position? (Laughter.)

DR. FRANKLIN: Right. I read that as the position of what Dr. Howard was advocating the university president *ought* to have as capability, whereas he and I are actually making pretty much the same point.

MR. HARDING: If I misjudged your intent, I apologize. I spent many years in the thirties arguing with Marxists and I found that they were capable of doing that sort of thing and I'm afraid I carried that over into the sixties.

MARVIN REDFIELD, National Aeronautics and Space Administration: I'd like to ask Dr. Franklin: If we can assume that there are some theories that you are perhaps affiliated with and perhaps even follow, do the students we are talking about really subscribe rather closely to the thoughts and the ideas that you have presented to us in the sessions that you have been here?

DR. FRANKLIN: I was talking about this at dinnertime and what I said to Dr. G. Warren Nutter, (coordinator of Rational Debates) was that my position is actually very much a minority position at this time. The position that I held, I would say, a year ago is much closer to the present majority position. Then I was talking to somebody else at dinner and said that when I presented my paper to some of the people I do work with, radical activists, they directly confronted the substance of the argument. I was impressed by the intellectual quality of their argument. They seized upon the weaker points in the argument. Since then, my argument has been strengthened because I've taken advantage of that discussion.

The subject that I'm dealing with and the approach, the method of analysis, is rapidly becoming the most important one, I think, within the radical left, particularly the radical left in relation to the universities. Does that answer the question?

MR. REDFIELD: I think it does. I'd like to ask a question vaguely related to that concerning your perception of the students who might be termed activists, loosely allied with your thinking. Let's say students who oppose or are, let's say, inert in this respect. Is there any differentiation that you have been able to make, since you live with these kids, as to which group, if any, has a clear idea as to what they would like to do after they get out of college? Is there any trend that you perceive as to whether one group or another has a clearer idea of what they would really like to do for their life's work following graduation? That's a question that I think perhaps bears on all of this problem.

DR. FRANKLIN: It's obvious to anybody who has been around the colleges and universities that the most alert students are having the greatest agonies about making that decision about what to do with their life. I don't know how I would put those two groups up against each other. I think there is a rapidly increasing number of the radical students who are making the decision that what they want to be is professional revolutionaries and that that would involve many different things.

For many of them it means getting a job, a working-class job, getting a job in a factory, not necessarily to stay in that particular factory but to learn from working people. A lot of the students, certainly at Stanford, do not come from working-class backgrounds and they feel very alienated from working people.

MR. REDFIELD: Is there a possible connection between the fact that these kinds of students might be very, very undecided as to what they ought to do and perhaps even frustrated about where they might plug into society, which might in fact lead them to these activist activities. Is there a relationship of any kind there?

DR. FRANKLIN: The way I would describe it is that these are people who have rejected the roles that they were supposed to have played. They have said at some point, "I don't want to do that. I don't want to be that."

The groups that I would compare are not the groups that you cite for comparison, but rather the group that is dropping out, that's going to the Haight-Ashbury or to the East Village or, I understand in Washington, to Georgetown. (Laughter.)

A VOICE: University?

DR. FRANKLIN: No, the area. (Laughter.)

Actually, I don't know about either one.

Those people I think have given up trying to make a decision. The others are in the process of making a decision.

There are many people now who are coming back out of that world and into the political activist world. As far as I can detect, and this is a very, very impressionistic judgment, what was predicted is not happening, that is, people coming in large numbers from the Haight and the East Village back into the straight life. Some are coming out of that into political life. Some are getting in very deep into destructive drugs and into a life style that's very self-destructive.

JULIUS DUSCHA, Washington Journalism Center: I think I know how Dr. Howard would like to run a university. I think he wants a strong president and a strong board of regents, despite some of his additional worry, but I am not at all sure in specifics what Dr. Franklin wants.

I would like to ask both of them to take a hypothetical case. You are going to start a university. Is it publicly or privately financed? How do you start it and how do you pick the board of regents or the governing body, whatever you want to call it? And please don't tell me that 80 percent of the people are working class because that includes just about all of us, I would guess, except Bert Harding's constituents here. (Laughter.) That's not my definition of the working class. I would like to get down to some specifics with both of you on the question up for debate. Also I would like to hear about the selection of faculty and students, once you get the governing board organized.

DR. FRANKLIN: I don't know if you've read the paper that I gave last week, or heard it.

MR. DUSCHA: I didn't. I was out of the—

DR. FRANKLIN: Or the discussion. We went around on that question several times, and I kept saying that I didn't want to engage in utopian speculation.

MR. DUSCHA: Let's take Stanford, which we both know something about. How would you re-do Stanford? If you don't want to start with University A, let's take Stanford. We're all aware of how that is operated now, I think.

DR. FRANKLIN: Let me just say the interesting thing to me is the way you phrase your questions. How do *"you"* set this up? How do *"you"* pick the governing body? Now, you didn't mean to come down on that "you" like that.

MR. DUSCHA: No. How should it be? How should it be selected?

DR. FRANKLIN: —one big difference between what Dr. Howard is doing, his method of analysis, and mine, is I am addressing myself directly to the question: Who should rule the universities? Whereas, I think the main thrust of his argument is: What should be the structural form of the university? Now, a lot of my analysis last week was an attempt to describe the evolution of the structure of the university. I am not interested in a hypothetical university; I am interested in the university that is evolving now, that is coming out of what I classify as the university of the bourgeoise.

MR. DUSCHA: You are talking about the working class and Eric Hoffer, with whom you would not agree on a lot of things, he also talks about the working class. He believes just as strongly as you do that he is of the working class, but you are far different in your views. So it seems to me you've got, at some point, to come down and say, All right, you're at Stanford University, it has to have some sort of a governing body, how should this governing body be picked? It can't take all the students that want to apply. How do you choose the students? These are the things I'd like to get down to from both of you.

DR. FRANKLIN: Again, those seem to be structuralist questions. I could give you specific answers, you see, about what *I* would like, what *I* think would be a good thing. I gave—

MR. DUSCHA: All right, let's have that.

DR. FRANKLIN: This is a transitional demand: Wherever there is a business school there should be a school set up of labor and community organizing. The people who teach in that school should be labor and community organizers with no regard to academic credentials.

MR. DUSCHA: Who picks the faculty? Who sets the faculty's duties?

DR. FRANKLIN: In order to run the universities in this society, whatever group it is has also to run the society as a whole. What I am particularly concerned with is developing grass roots participatory democracy, organs of power for the people to effect their will. That's my definition of freedom. Now they may pick one structure for a university over here and another structure over there. I don't think it really makes any difference. One may work a little bit better than the other one and that will be tested in practice. But the structural question I don't think is at all to the point.

MR. DUSCHA: Who does pick the faculty? We now know the faculty of the school of business at Stanford is picked largely or certainly with the veto power of the dean of the school. Who would pick the faculty of your school of this Saul Alinsky Memorial School of Organizers? (Laughter.) Or the Bruce Franklin Memorial School? (Laughter.)

DR. FRANKLIN: Heaven forbid. I think that the university should be intimately integrated with the surrounding community and that whatever participatory organs of power are in that surrounding community should be making the decisions about how the faculty is selected. That, I think, answers the question directly.

MR. DUSCHA: Take Stanford. What is the participatory community?

A VOICE: Hewlett Packard is. (Laughter.)

ANOTHER VOICE: He's sponsored by the government.

DR. FRANKLIN: Yes, that's what it is right now. I think that what it should be is people who work in the plants, whose directors are now also the trustees of Stanford, the people who work in the electronic industry there, the people who live in East Palo Alto, which is the black ghetto, the Chicano people of San Jose, these are the people. They are the ones who should do the picking.

Now, there is no doubt about what the situation is at present.

MR. DUSCHA: I am seeking what you want to do. I'll accept some of your argument at present, much of it, in fact. But I am still puzzled. You know, George Wallace was participatory democracy.

DR. FRANKLIN: Not really. I mean, H. L. Hunt ain't participatory democracy.

MR. DUSCHA: McCarthy was participatory democracy, but these are quite different things. If the participatory democrats in the Palo Alto area said, We want a George Wallace type school, you would accept this?

DR. FRANKLIN: I would argue against that. That's all I can say. Given the fact that people have power, it's also clear that some of their decisions will be wrong decisions, any way you want to look at them. They are going to make mistakes. I think it's the duty of everybody who thinks that they are making a mistake to say so, to argue for his position, to say George Wallace doesn't really represent us, for such and such reasons, look at Alabama and so on, look at H. L. Hunt or whatever.

DR. HOWARD: May I answer?

MR. DUSCHA: I'm sorry but let me ask Mr. Franklin one other thing. Do you assume that an institution has to have a board of governors, a president or does it just kind of run itself?

DR. FRANKLIN: I don't think that it necessarily does have to have a board of governors. I think that there are many different organizational structures which ought to be experimented with to see which work best.

MR. DUSCHA: Name two, say.

DR. FRANKLIN: One would be a plebiscite on major questions. Another would be a high degree of autonomy for different areas within the university. One would be—

MR. DUSCHA: Which there is in fact now at—

DR. FRANKLIN: Maybe the school of engineering should be responsible directly to such and such a group of people who are directly affected by the decisions made there, rather than trying to get everybody involved in decisions.

MR. DUSCHA: Who should the school of engineering be responsible to?

DR. FRANKLIN: As I said before, it's to the people who work in the plants that are tied in with it and the people who are serviced by its product. That gets much larger.

MR. DUSCHA: That really is everybody, isn't it?

DR. FRANKLIN: It depends on which department—

MR. DUSCHA: We all buy automobiles.

DR. HOWARD: Bruce, I think that you've contaminated me because my answer to this is also an idealogue answer. The point of my paper was to support the most completely pluralistic system of higher education possible. I am delighted that the Baptists have developed a series of Baptist colleges and the states have developed their own colleges. I would like to see Saul Alinsky and Bruce Franklin develop their college.

It seems to me that this is what this country is all about the interrelationships would be different one from the next. I still maintain that an educational institution is so complex that there has to be somebody who is trying to keep in touch with the different elements of it and trying to make certain that the thing doesn't simply become what I think many institutions have become, a whole lot of separately operating units with no framework of common reference and no common purpose.

This, I think, is essential if you are going to be concerned about what happens to the students in the institution rather than, as seems to be happening now, having a number of institutions primarily concerned with the production of knowledge. (Applause.)

MR. ALEXANDER: I wanted to ask each man to say something about morality, by which I mean not prohibition of actions but in the positive way, social obligations. It seems to me that every university commenced with a social obligation. The community says, "We want to help the people here," or the church said so or, I think in the case of Johns Hopkins, maybe the scientific profession said so. So there is that morality there.

To me that kind of morality includes tolerance of other people's ideas, other people's religions, other people's communities. I think there is a great difference between these two men in the interpretation of that kind of morality. Tolerance is the key word.

DR. HOWARD: Yes, I'm for tolerance. I'm not being facetious.

MR. ALEXANDER: No.

DR. HOWARD: It seems to me that this is a characteristic that I've been trying to drive at.

MR. ALEXANDER: You want pluralistic tolerance.

DR. HOWARD: That's right. Protected.

DR. FRANKLIN: I think that this pluralistic tolerance is a tolerance only of one small group really, as far as control over the educational institutions is concerned. In other words, you need enormous resources of wealth and power in order to set up a university or in order to keep a university going. So to say "Go set up your own pluralistic university" is preposterous.

DR. HOWARD: But we have them.

DR. FRANKLIN: And they are all—

DR. HOWARD: The Quakers, the Presbyterians, the Baptists, the Catholics, the—

DR. FRANKLIN: But if you go down the universities in this country they are overwhelmingly run by corporate capitalists. They are the ones who sit on the boards of trustees and the boards of regents and make the fundamental decisions from which all day-to-day decisions flow.

MR. ALEXANDER: When you reach the top of the group, the head at least of the top of the centristic pyramid, I see what you are talking about.

DR. FRANKLIN: You see, it's cruel—

MR. ALEXANDER: It's intolerant.

DR. FRANKLIN: It's cruel to say to poor people or working people, "Go set up your own university."

MR. ALEXANDER: But it's been done. It's been done.

DR. FRANKLIN: The university that we're talking about is one that has a huge library, that has fantastic technological equipment, that has many classrooms, that has the power to hire people so that they can live in an inflationary society.

JAMES GALLAGHER: The same committee, I believe. (Laughter.)

I was here two weeks ago and listened to Mr. Howard and he drew a very, very tight case, I thought, for the purpose and function of a university. I think we are talking now about who should pick the faculty and so forth. But he pointed out the university's main and principal function was to pursue the truth and the by-product or secondary purpose was dissemination of that truth. About a half hour ago the other gentleman pointed out that the university and the faculty are servants of the people. It seems to me that in the case of a university you can't serve two masters, chasing both the truth and students. I know that the students have been chasing around Stanford today when the SDS chapter had their Vietcong flag full time but I'm not talking about that.

Who then should pursue the truth? We have a lot of servants of the people. The government is the biggest service organization going. There are 13 million people working for the government, national, state, and local governments in the United States, in addition to many private groups.

Wouldn't it be something if those 13 million people became the ones to pursue truth? This would throw a real crimp into people like Bobby Baker and open all kinds of moonlighting possibilities.

I submit that on the function of the university there is a definite division here of thinking. A university, in my opinion, is not the servant of students. Perhaps the students seek out universities because they know the faculty members are in search of truth and they migrate to them for that reason.

DR. FRANKLIN: I think that everybody in this society ought to be engaged in the pursuit of truth and I think that the universities should be in the process, as indeed they are, of liberating the masses of people within the society. I don't think you should have a society in which some people say, "I pursue truth, those people over there, they are supposed to stay home and look at their television sets or whatever they do."

DR. PENNIMAN: Mr. Franklin is back again, it seems to me, at the game we were playing all last week, which was discussed earlier this evening, of making the definitions up as we go along to fit the particular argument being dealt with. Part of the time you are talking about the working class. The last time around when you were talking about the working class you were talking about blue-collar, mechanical-type workers as opposed to the ones that we were talking about when there were 80 percent. When you talk about who is in the left that turns out to be the most alert students, which I am sure must be true by definition, given your position.

Earlier you asserted that political scientists and economic departments are really outside this world of analysis that you deal in. Here are the experts in the field but you have some set aside from your analytical world. Yet here are the ones who deal with these problems all of the time and who have worked at it for their whole adult lives in most cases, and, for the most part, you don't find a Marxist among them. Virtually none that I know of—I can think of one or two in the economics profession — (laughter) — we happily are more free of them. But, even so, there are very few.

I am reminded therefore of the comments that are made in a book written by one of your colleagues,

Gabriel Almond, on the appeals of communism. It is suggested there that one of the great attractions of the Marxist position is that it allows everyone to become an instant scientist. The world begins to or has to fit into the simplistic view of history, which in turn then solves all of your problems because it has to come out this way, aided, to be sure, by the party or by the intellectuals who are leading it or by some other group. And this too in general fits.

I think the efforts that have been made tonight make it clear that one can't argue with you because, as long as your system is closed, there is no way to get into it, even on these very practical questions that have been asked you here by Mr. Duscha and by others. You simply avoid them.

To get out of this closed system, then, it seems to me, one is faced with the same kinds of problems that Victor Sayres was talking about when he was talking about the noises that he heard in the prisons of the country. In your particular case it would seem to me that you are going to get involved in listening to the hacks and the opportunists. The party at some time will drive you out because you happen to have the advantage of not being in. You have stayed on the outside and played a fellow traveler role as a professional revolutionist without really being a professional revolutionist. You will argue, I think practically enough, that this is an ad hominem argument.

But it is an ad hominem argument because, in fact, there is no way you can avoid it in dealing with this kind of a problem. The best one can do is to speak to the rest of the audience because you can't deal with the problem, you won't deal with it.

So you have asked them before "why don't you meet it head on?" And they have met it head on and you ignored it. Or you have said, "All right, let's deal with something else." They have tried to deal with facts and you won't allow them to deal with facts. There is virtually no way that one can meet an argument with you because you insist upon letting it go by. Let me just simply close this discussion about the question by saying that happily there are not very many working-class revolutionaries or they are sufficiently few in number so that it probably isn't going to make much difference. I suppose this is the bright part.

DR. FRANKLIN: I didn't hear that.

DR. PENNIMAN: I said, fortunately the numbers whom you represent are so small that aside from a certain amount of entertainment that one gets out of listening and re-listening to what one heard in the thirties with no advance so far as I can tell, there isn't much impact that it has upon society.

DR. FRANKLIN: Well, you can keep kidding yourself. Now as far as the two points that you accuse me of shifting terms on or of manipulating, I think I can show very clearly that you are the one who is doing that. First you accused me of switching from a definition of worker as blue-collar worker to a definition of worker as blue-collar and white-collar worker. Let me remind you that the term blue-collar worker was introduced by somebody who questioned me last time, who insisted that the bulk of Wallace's support had come from blue-collar workers.

Second, you said that I said that the most alert students were the left-wing students. What I said in fact was that the most alert students were the ones who are having the most agonizing time of making a career decision. I did not make it political.

DR. PENNIMAN: The choice being whether they would be revolutionaries or not.

DR. FRANKLIN: No, no, no. You misunderstood what I was saying—or something. As to the statement you make about political science and economic departments, that you don't find a Marxist among them, I would agree, though you had one or two exceptions. I think that that clearly shows that the pretended neutrality of this ideology in the university is precisely that, a pretense, because you can go to other societies where all of the economists are Marxists or claim to be. (Laughter.)

There are reasons for that. Part of it has to do with who is doing the hiring of the faculty, who is running the university, which is exactly what we're talking about.

A VOICE: Where is that evidence on the Wallace vote you said you would produce?

DR. FRANKLIN: Okay, I'll read you the whole footnote.

Last week angry shouts of protest greeted my assertion that Wallace's main support did not come from blue-collar workers as was stated, but rather was in general directly proportional to the income and education of the electorate in different neighborhoods. I was challenged to produce evidence.

I refer you to *The New York Times* of November 6, 1968, pages 1 and 23, and November 8, 1968, page 27. One analyst for the *Times*—this is in the first article— was quite surprised to discover that the neighborhoods which were supposed to go heavily for Wallace, those where there were heavy concentrations of Irish, Polish, and Italian blue-collar workers, had given him negligible support. One example he cited was the closely-watched second district of Buffalo's 7th ward, which is almost completely made up of Polish blue-collar workers. They gave Wallace a grand total of 36 votes out of 588 cast. The same article cites evidence that over 50 percent of the Wallace vote outside the South came from Republicans. The *Times'* statistical breakdown of the vote in New York City and its suburbs is very clear.

The Wallace vote in New York City as a whole was a mere 4 percent, with Richmond, the middle-class suburban borough, giving by far the highest percentage, 9 percent, compared to 3 percent in Manhattan, 5 percent in the Bronx, 4 percent in Brooklyn, and 6 percent in Queens.

Nassau County gave Wallace 5 percent. Westchester County 6 percent, that is, 50 percent higher than New York City, and Suffolk County gave him 9 percent, a little more than double the New York City percentage.

The area-by-area breakdown is even more instructive. For instance, New York City's 60th assembly district, heavily populated by Italian blue-collar workers, it includes Little Italy, gave Wallace 4 percent. This compares strikingly with the vote in the wealthy Long Island communities of Southhampton, 9 percent, Southold, 9½ percent, and Riverhead, 12½ percent.

But even if the working class had voted more heavily for Wallace, what would that prove about who should run the universities? Wallace was the only highly-publicized candidate, that is, publicized by the ruling-class press, with a working class background and the only one attacking corporate power, although that, as with Hitler, was a hoax.

DR. HOWARD: Referring to the same source, the national statistics on that question, *New York Times* December 8 said that 15 percent of the manual laborers voted for Wallace, 5 percent of Republicans, 14 percent of Democrats.

DR. FRANKLIN: Let me point out that that is a Gallup Poll. I am familiar with that Gallup Poll. One of my points is that the polls are manipulative and false.

If you look at the actual vote, not the polls, you will find quite the reverse of that propaganda because, for one thing, in the polls they don't go into poor neighborhoods and they don't go into black neighborhoods.

DR. HOWARD: He's correct. It is the report of *The New York Times* by the Gallup Election Analysis.

In a summary statement I would like to say I find it difficult, as have other members of this audience, to respond intelligently to Dr. Franklin's position. I am certain that a significant part of my failure there is my limited understanding of Marxism. I am sincere in saying this.

But I do believe that you, Dr. Franklin, don't understand our society. For instance, when you talk about workingmen. Dr. Harold Passer, an economist in Rochester, says that over the past century the productivity of the American workingman has increased about 2 percent a year, as has his real adjusted-for-inflation pay. During the same period the real return on capital has remained about constant. Except for medical and dental service available to him, the position of the capitalist has not improved in the last century.

Furthermore, I read an article which intrigued me which showed a statistical analysis of the working hours of the industrial executive. Certainly, in recent years in this country, the workingman's hours have shortened and the executive's hours have lengthened. Medical statistics on people who have worked themselves into illness—and I realize that there is worry involved in this too—are much higher for the corporate officers than for the average workingman. It seems to me that our system is one which has progressively helped the poorer elements in the society, certainly imperfectly and slowly. But over a period of time it is the workingman whose relative position has been improved most.

Secondly, it seems to me it's very easy, and I am sure you are sincere in doing this, for you to put a label on something and to assume that that solves the question. For instance, you spoke about law and justice. We had a really extraordinary speech given on our campus by Morris Liebman, an attorney in Chicago. He was then the chairman of President Johnson's Committee to Evaluate the Poverty Program and he spoke on the subject of law. He said every time he goes to a campus to talk about law the students want to talk about justice. He said there is not and never can be any justice of any kind for anyone or any group without a prior commitment to a system of law. He said that in this country we have developed the most extraordinary legal system for developing more and more justice that man has ever created. We have the United States Congress which spends full time changing laws to try to bring about more justice. We have a Supreme Court that works full time trying to interpret laws for justice. We have a significant part of the time of the executive directed toward proposing laws to bring about more justice and we have counterparts for those in every state in the country and in every smaller governmental region.

In our kind of society it is a slow-moving thing because it does work by democratic processes. But the difference is that all of the people have a chance to have a part in it or a large portion of them do. In a dictatorship change can be swift and it can be efficient, perhaps, but again the justice is what the dictator judges.

It seems to me that this has been a discussion between two men whose remarks largely went by each other because, as you recognized and I recognized, you begin with a view of man and how he can best serve in a society and I begin with a very different view of what mankind is and how he can be best served in society. I think that if you back off far enough you will see that this is an inevitable failure of confrontation. I feel that it's been a very useful failure and I appreciate the chance to take part in it. (Applause.)

DR. FRANKLIN: Let me say I think that people who say that *you* can't argue with my argument are absolutely correct. (Laughter.) I have said over and over again ideological knowledge can only serve the class that produced it, to whom it is meant to be useful. My argument can be argued with but that would have to be by people who share, I think, the basic loyalties and values that I share. That's why I got a much tougher argument from the student radicals to whom I presented this paper.

So I think we ought to recognize that we have two ideological systems confronting each other. It may very well be that you cannot have rational dialogue between them. There is the statement of one position and a statement of the other position and then one chooses sides.

Somebody asked last week the facetious question: Aren't you worried that now that you have given the blueprint for change the power structure will deal with it by taking the other option? In replying, I pointed to the objective limitations on the options available to the ruling class.

Given the fact that I think most people here, as Dr. Howard very frankly says, are not conversant with Marxism, I would like to make something very clear. Marxists do not say "capitalism is bad; communism is good." They say capitalism is good up to a point, that it is capitalism which, through competition, yes, has released the productive resources that enable man to meet his material needs, that we had to go. through capitalism. It produced a technology which was fantastic. Marx described capitalism's constant revolutionizing of production, which remains very important. Marxism is not for some static utopia. But when capitalism develops to a certain point its internal contradictions make it increasingly irrational.

I further would argue that the bourgeois university is good insofar as it has developed. insofar as it has been able to meet some real human needs on a large scale.

I am not for going back to some primal, beautiful university that never existed. As a Marxist, I see my obligation to give an analysis of the processes of change that are going on within that university itself; my argument was pointed to certain actual basic changes. One, you have vastly increased and increasing enrollment, which means a widening class basis for the student body and also a widening class basis for the younger faculty. Then you have—and this is not reversible—an increasing inter-penetration of the giant university, the multiversity, with the other major economic and political and social institutions of the society.

At the same time you have a rapidly generating technology within that university. Another change which is a product of this is that you have rapidly increasing demands being made on the university, demands of widening numbers of people to be serviced by the university, and to participate in the university as students but also as people who make decisions about what that university should be doing.

My answer to the question: Who should run the university? is that analysis of the actual processes that I see going on. (Applause.)

FOOTNOTES

FIRST LECTURE

[1] Walter Lippmann, "The University and the Human Condition," *Whose Goals for American Higher Education?*, ed., Dobbins and Lee (Washington: American Council on Education, 1968), pp. 233-34.

SECOND LECTURE

[1] *San Francisco Chronicle*, January 2, 1969.

[2] Clark Kerr, *The Uses of the University* (Harvard University Press, 1964), p. 20.

[3] *Ibid.*, pp. 7-8.

[4] *Ibid.*, p. 87.

[5] *Ibid.*, p. 88.

[6] On Stanford, see David Ransom, "The Stanford Complex" in "The University at War" issue of *Viet Report* (January, 1968) and *Through the Looking Glass: A Radical Guide to Stanford*, put out by Stanford SDS in 1968.

[7] Ransom, *op. cit.*, p. 19.

[8] *Ibid.*

[9] There is an erroneous implication here, because I have since learned that Stanford's board is also deeply involved in California agro-business. Tenneco Oil, for one, owns the huge Kern County Land Company, one of the struck grape growers.

[10] Marvin Garson and Ken Blum, *The Regents* (Berkeley, 1967).

[11] *San Francisco Chronicle*, January 7, 1969.

[12] See the recent survey of the nation's trustees conducted by the Educational Testing Service. The survey reveals that the typical trustee is white, Protestant, in his 50s, and occupies a prestige position in business. He favors loyalty oaths, thinks that the faculty should not have major authority in appointing

their academic dean, and wishes to share his decision-making power only with the administration. (*San Francisco Chronicle*, January 12, 1969.)

[13] Jerry Farber, "Students are Niggers," reprinted in *Stanford Daily*, October 8, 1968.

[14] *Lenin on Youth* (Moscow: Progress Publishers, 1967), pp. 103-04.

[15] *Ibid.*, pp. 131-34.

[16] *Ibid.*, p. 135.

[17] "Manifesto of the Communist Party" in *The Essential Left* (New York: Barnes and Noble, 1963), p. 17.

[18] Carl Davidson, "The Multiversity: Crucible of the New Working Class" (SDS, n.d.), p. 7.

REBUTTALS

H. BRUCE FRANKLIN

[1] Last week angry shouts of protest greeted my assertion that Wallace's main support did not come from blue-collar workers, but rather was in general directly proportional to the income and education of the electorate in different neighborhoods; and I was challenged to produce evidence. I refer you to *The New York Times*, November 6, 1968, pp. 1, 23, and November 8, 1968, p. 27. One analyst for the *Times* was quite surprised to discover that the neighborhoods which were supposed to go heavily for Wallace, those where there were heavy concentrations of Irish, Polish, and Italian blue-collar workers, had given him negligible support. One example he cited was the closely-watched 2d District of Buffalo's 7th Ward, which is almost completely made up of Polish blue-collar workers; they gave Wallace a grand total of 36 votes out of 588 cast (6 percent). The same article cites evidence that over 50 percent of the Wallace vote outside the South came from Republicans. The *Times*' statistical breakdown of the vote in New York City and its suburbs is very clear. The Wallace vote in New York City as a whole was a mere 4 percent, with Richmond, the middle-class suburban borough, giving by far the highest percentage (9 percent, compared to 3 percent in Manhattan, 5 percent in the Bronx, 4 percent in Brooklyn, and 6 percent in Queens). Nassau County gave Wallace 5 percent, Westchester County 6 percent, that is 50 percent higher than New York City, and Suffolk County gave him 9 percent, well more than double the New York City percentage. The area by area breakdown is even more instructive. For instance, New York City's 60th Assembly District, heavily populated by Italian blue-collar workers (it includes "Little Italy"), gave Wallace 4 percent; this compares strikingly with the vote in the wealthy Long Island communities of Southampton (9 percent), Southold (9½ percent), and Riverhead (12½ percent).

But even if the working class had voted more heavily for Wallace, what would that prove about who should run the universities? Wallace was the only highly-publicized candidate with a working-class background, and the only one attacking corporate power (although that, as with Hitler, was a hoax).

Sit-downs are strikes. Such strikers are clearly trespassers and violators of the law of the land. We cannot have bona fide collective bargaining with sit-down strikers in illegal possession of plants. Collective bargaining cannot be justified if one party, having seized the plant, holds a gun at the other party's head.

William S. Knudsen, Executive Vice President of General Motors

It is unfortunate when a handful of strangers can meet in Washington and then in Detroit to determine courses of action and even create demands that result in idleness for thousands of contented workers and disrupt a happy community.

Harlow Curtice, President of Buick Motor Co.

[3] This sentence originally read: "Dr. Howard gives it all away when he names the first qualification of his ideal university president." But in the ensuing discussion I discovered that I had misunderstood Dr. Howard's point.